The Writings of Methodius

The Writings of Methodius

The Writings of Methodius

© Lighthouse Publishing 2024

Written by: Methodius (AD 260 - 312)
Translated by: Rev. William R. Clark, M.A. (1829 – 1912)
Updated into Modern U.S English: A.M. Overett (b.1960)

All rights reserved. Without limiting the rights under copyright reserved above, no part of this publication may be reproduced, stored in a retrieval system, or transmitted, in any form or by any means (electronic, mechanical, photocopying, recording or otherwise), without the prior written permission of the copyright owner of this book.

Published by
Lighthouse Publishing
SAN 257-4330
228 Freedom Parkway
Hoschton, GA 30548
United States of America

www.lighthousechristianpublishing.com

Introductory Notice
To
Methodius.

[a.d. 260–312]. Considering the strong language in which Methodius is praised by ancient writers, as well as by the moderns, I feel that our learned translator has too hastily dismissed his name and works in the biographical introduction below. Epiphanius makes great use of him in his refutations of Origen; and Dupin's critical and historical notice of him is prolonged and highly discriminating, furnishing an abridgment of all his writings and of those vulgarly attributed to him heretofore. I have made into an elucidation some references which may be of use to the student. In like manner, I have thrown into the form of notes and elucidations what would be less pertinent and less useful in a preface. There are no facts to be added to what is here given by the translator; and remarks on the several works, which he has too sparingly annotated, will be more conveniently bestowed, perhaps, on the pages to which they immediately refer. The following is the translator's brief but useful

Introduction.

Methodius, who is also called Eubulius, was, first of all bishop, simultaneously of Olympus and Patara, in Lycia, as is testified by several ancient writers. He was afterwards removed, according to St. Jerome, to the episcopal See of Tyre in Phoenicia, and at the end of the latest of the great persecutions of the Church, about the year 312, he suffered martyrdom at Chalcis in Greece. Some consider that it was at Chalcis in Syria, and that St. Jerome's testimony ought to be thus understood, as Syria was more likely to be the scene of his martyrdom that Greece, as being nearer to his diocese. Others affirm that he suffered under Decius and Valerian; but this is incorrect, since he wrote not only against Origen long after the death of Adamantius, but also against Porphyry, whilst he was alive, in the reign of Diocletian.

Methodius is known chiefly as the antagonist of Origen; although, as has been pointed out, he was himself influenced in no small degree by the method of Origen, as may be seen by his tendency to allegorical interpretations of Holy Scripture. The only complete work of this writer which has come down to us is his *Banquet of the Ten Virgins*, a dialogue of considerable power and grace, in praise of the virginal life. His antagonism to Origen, however, comes out less in this than in his works *On the Resurrection*, and *On Things Created*. The treatise *On Free Will* is, according to recent critics, of doubtful authorship, although the internal evidence must be said to confirm the ancient testimonies which assign it to Methodius. His writings against Porphyry, with the exception of some slight fragments, are lost, as are also his exegetical writings.

Combefis published an edition of his works in 1644; but only so much of the *Banquet* as was contained in the *Bibliotheca* of Photius. In 1656 Leo Allatius published for the first time a complete edition of this work at Rome from the Vatican ms. Combefis in 1672 published an edition founded chiefly upon this; and his work has become the basis of all subsequent reprints.

The following translation has been made almost entirely from the text of Migne, which is generally accurate, and the arrangement of which has been followed throughout. The edition of Jahn in some places rearranges the more fragmentary works, especially that *On the Resurrection*; but, although his text was occasionally found useful in amending the old readings, and in improving the punctuation, it was thought better to adhere in general to the text which is best known.

A writer who was pronounced by St. Epiphanius to be "a learned man and a most valiant defender of the truth," and by St. Jerome, *disertissimus martyr*, who elsewhere speaks of him as one who *nitidi compositique sermonis libros confecit*, cannot be altogether unworthy the attention of the nineteenth century.

The Banquet of the Ten Virgins;
Or,
Concerning Chastity.

Persons of the Dialogue: Euboulios, Gregorion, Arete; Marcella, Theophila, Thaleia, Theopatra, Thallousa, Agathe, Procilla, Thekla, Tusiane, Domnina.

Introduction.—Plan of the Work; Way to Paradise; Description and Personification of Virtue; The Agnos a Symbol of Chastity; Marcella, the Eldest and Foremost Among the Virgins of Christ.

Euboulios. You have arrived most seasonably, Gregorion, for I have just been looking for you, wanting to hear of the meeting of Marcella and Theopatra, and of the other virgins who were present at the banquet, and of the nature of their discourses on the subject of chastity; for it is said that they argued with such ability and power that there was nothing lacking to the full consideration of the subject. If, therefore, you have come here for any other purpose, put that off to another time, and do not delay to give us a complete and connected account of the matter of which we are inquiring.

Gregorion. I seem to be disappointed of my hope, as someone else has given you intelligence beforehand on the subject respecting which you ask me. For I thought that you had heard nothing of what had happened, and I was flattering myself greatly with the idea that I should be the first to tell you of it. And for this reason I made all haste to come here to you, fearing the very thing which has happened, that someone might anticipate me.

Euboulios. Be comforted, my excellent friend, for we have had no precise information respecting anything which happened; since the person who brought us the intelligence had nothing to tell us, except that there had been dialogues; but when he was asked what they were, and to what purpose, he did not know.

Gregorion. Well then, as I came here for this reason, do you want to hear all that was said from the beginning; or shall I pass by parts of it, and recall only those points which I consider worthy of mention?

Euboulios. By no means the latter; but first, Gregorion, relate to us from the very beginning where the meeting was, and about the setting forth of the viands, and about yourself, how you poured out the wine

"They in golden cups
Each other pledged, while towards broad heaven they looked."

Gregorion. You are always skillful in discussions, and excessively powerful in argument—thoroughly confuting all your adversaries.

Euboulios. It is not worthwhile, Gregorion, to contend about these things at present; but do oblige us by simply telling us what happened from the beginning.

Gregorion. Well, I will try. But first answer me this: You know, I presume, Arete, the daughter of Philosophia?

Euboulios. Why do you ask?

Gregorion. "We went by invitation to a garden of hers with an eastern aspect, to enjoy the fruits of the season, myself, and Procilla, and Tusiane." I am repeating the words of Theo patra, for it was of her I obtained the information. "We went, Gregorion, by a very rough, steep, and arduous path: when we drew near to the place," said Theopatra, "we were met by a tall and beautiful woman walking along quietly and gracefully, clothed in a shining robe as white as snow. Her beauty was something altogether inconceivable and divine. Modesty, blended with majesty, bloomed on her countenance. It was a face," she said, "such as I know not that I had ever seen, awe-inspiring, yet tempered with gentleness and mirth; for it was wholly unadorned by art, and had nothing counterfeit. She came up to us, and, like a mother who sees her daughters after a long separation, she embraced and kissed each one of us with great joy, saying, 'O, my daughters, you have come with toil and pain to me who am earnestly longing to conduct you to the pasture of immortality; toilsomely have you come by a way abounding with many frightful reptiles; for, as I looked, I saw you often stepping aside, and I was fearing lest you should turn back and slip over the precipices. But thanks to the Bridegroom to whom I have espoused you, my children, for having granted an effectual answer to all our prayers.' And, while she is thus speaking," said Theopatra, "we arrive at the enclosure, the doors not being shut as yet, and as we enter we come upon Thekla and Agathe and Marcella preparing to sup. And Arete immediately said, 'Do you also come hither, and sit down here in your place along with these your fellows.' Now," said she to me, "we who were there as guests were altogether, I think, ten in number; and the place was marvelously beautiful, and abounding in the means of recreation. The air was diffused in soft and regular currents, mingled with pure beams of light, and a stream flowing as gently as oil through the very middle of the garden, threw up a most delicious drink; and the water flowing from it, transparent and pure, formed itself into fountains, and these, overflowing like rivers, watered all the garden with their abundant streams; and there were different kinds of trees there, full of fresh fruits, and the fruits that hung joyfully from their branches were of equal beauty; and there were ever-blooming meadows strewn with variegated and sweet-scented flowers, from which came a gentle breeze laden with sweetest odor. And the agnos grew near, a lofty tree, under which we reposed, from its being exceedingly wide-spreading and shady."

Euboulios. You seem to me, my good friend, to be making a revelation of a second paradise.

Gregorion. You speak truly and wisely. "When there," she said, "we had all kinds of food and a variety of festivities, so that no delight was wanting. After this Arete, entering, gave utterance to these words:—

"'Young maidens, the glory of my greatness, beautiful virgins, who tend the undefiled meadows of Christ with unwedded hands, we have now had enough of food and feasting, for all things are abundant and plentiful with us. What is there, then, besides which I wish and expect? That each of you shall pronounce a discourse in praise of virginity. Let Marcella begin, since she sits in the highest place, and is at the same time the eldest. I shall be ashamed of myself if I do not make the successful disputant an object of envy, binding her with the unfading flowers of wisdom.'

"And then," I think she said, "Marcella immediately began to speak as follows."

Discourse I.—Marcella.

Chapter I.—The Difficulty and Excellence of Virginity; The Study of Doctrine Necessary for Virgins.

Virginity is something supernaturally great, wonderful, and glorious; and, to speak plainly and in accordance with the Holy Scriptures, this best and noblest manner of life alone is the root of immortality, and also its flower and first-fruits; and for this reason the Lord promises that those shall enter into the kingdom of heaven who have made themselves eunuchs, in that passage of the Gospels in which He lays down the various reasons for which men have made themselves eunuchs. Chastity with men is a very rare thing, and difficult of attainment, and in proportion to its supreme excellence and magnificence is the greatness of its dangers.

For this reason, it requires strong and generous natures, such as, vaulting over the stream of pleasure, direct the chariot of the soul upwards from the earth, not turning aside from their aim, until having, by swiftness of thought, lightly bounded above the world, and taken their stand truly upon the vault of heaven, they purely contemplate immortality itself as it springs forth from the undefiled bosom of the Almighty.

Earth could not bring forth this draught; heaven alone knew the fountain from whence it flows; for we must think of virginity as walking indeed upon the earth, but as also reaching up to heaven. And hence some who have longed for it, and considering only the end of it, have come, by reason of coarseness of mind, ineffectually with unwashed feet, and have gone aside out of the way, from having conceived no worthy idea of the *virginal* manner of life. For it is not enough to keep the body only undefiled, just as we should not show that we think more of the temple than of the image of the god; but we should care for the souls of men as being the divinities of their bodies, and adorn them with righteousness. And then do they most care for them and tend them when, striving untiringly to hear divine discourses, they do not desist until, wearing the doors of the wise, they attain to the knowledge of the truth.

For as the putrid humors and matter of flesh, and all those things which corrupt it, are driven out by salt, in the same manner all the irrational appetites of a virgin are banished from the body by divine teaching. For it must needs be that the soul which is not sprinkled with the words of Christ, as with salt, should stink and breed worms, as King David, openly confessing with tears in the mountains, cried out, "My wounds stink and are corrupt," because he had not salted himself with the exercises of self-control, and so subdued his carnal appetites, but self-indulgently had yielded to them, and became corrupted in adultery. And hence, in Leviticus, every gift, unless it be seasoned with salt, is forbidden to be offered as an oblation to the Lord God. Now the whole spiritual meditation of the Scriptures is given to us as salt which stings in order to benefit, and which disinfects, without which it is impossible for a soul, by means of reason, to be brought to the Almighty; for "ye are the salt of the earth," said the Lord to the apostles. It is fitting, then, that a virgin should always love things which are honorable, and be distinguished among the foremost for wisdom and addicted to nothing slothful or luxurious, but should excel, and set her mind upon things worthy of the state of virginity, always putting away, by the word, the foulness of luxury, lest in any way some slight hidden corruption should breed the worm of incontinence; for "the unmarried woman cares for the things of the Lord," how she may please the Lord, "that she may be holy both in body and in spirit," says the blessed Paul. But many of them who consider the hearing of the word quite a secondary matter, think they do great things if they give their attention to it for a little while. But discrimination must be exercised with respect to these; for it is not fitting to impart divine instruction to a nature which is careful about trifles, and low, and which counterfeits wisdom. For would it not be laughable to go on talking to those who direct all their energy towards things of little value, in order that they may complete most accurately those things which they want to bring to perfection, but do not think that the greatest pains are to be taken with those necessary things by which most of all the love of chastity would be increased in them?

Chapter II.—Virginity a Plant from Heaven, Introduced Late; The Advancement of Mankind to Perfection, How Arranged.

For truly by a great stretch of power the plant of virginity was sent down to men from heaven, and for this reason it was not revealed to the first generations. For the race of mankind was still very small in number; and it was necessary that it should first be increased in number, and then brought to perfection. Therefore the men of old times thought it nothing unseemly to take their own sisters for wives, until the law coming separated them, and by forbidding that which at first had seemed to be right, declared it to be a sin, calling him cursed who should "uncover the nakedness" of his sister; God thus mercifully bringing to our race the needful help in due season, as parents do to their children. For they do not at once set masters over them, but allow them, during the period of childhood, to amuse themselves like young animals, and first send them to teachers stammering like themselves, until they cast off the youthful wool of the mind, and go onwards to the practice of greater things, and from thence again to that of greater still. And thus we must consider that the God and Father of all acted towards our forefathers. For the world, while still unfilled with men, was like a child, and it was necessary that it should first be filled with these, and so grow to manhood. But when hereafter it was colonized from end to end, the race of man spreading to a boundless extent, God no longer allowed man to remain in the same ways, considering how they might now proceed from one point to another, and advance nearer to heaven, until, having attained to the very greatest and most exalted lesson of virginity, they should reach to perfection; that first they should abandon the intermarriage of brothers and sisters, and marry wives from other families; and then that they should no longer have many wives, like brute beasts, as though born for the mere propagation of the species; and then that they should not be adulterers; and then again that they should go on to continence, and from continence to virginity, when, having trained themselves to despise the flesh, they sail fearlessly into the peaceful haven of immortality.

Chapter III.—By the Circumcision of Abraham, Marriage with Sisters Forbidden; In the Times of the Prophets Polygamy Put a Stop To; Conjugal Purity Itself by Degrees Enforced.

If, however, any one should venture to find fault with our argument as destitute of Scripture proof, we will bring forward the writings of the prophets, and more fully demonstrate the truth of the statements already made. Now Abraham, when he first received the covenant of circumcision, seems to signify, by receiving circumcision in a member of his own body, nothing else than this, that one should no longer beget children with one born of the same parent; showing that everyone should abstain from intercourse with his own sister, as his own flesh. And thus, from the time of Abraham, the custom of marrying with sisters has ceased; and from the times of the prophets the contracting of marriage with several wives has been done away with; for we read, "Go not after thy lusts, but refrain thyself from thine appetites;" for "wine and women will make men of understanding to fall away;" and in another place, "Let thy fountain be blessed; and rejoice with the wife of thy youth," manifestly forbidding a plurality of wives. And Jeremiah clearly gives the name of "fed horses" to those who lust after other women; and we read, "The multiplying brood of the ungodly shall not thrive, nor take deep rooting from bastard slips, nor lay any fast foundation."

Lest, however, we should seem prolix in collecting the testimonies of the prophets, let us again point out how chastity succeeded to marriage with one wife, taking away by degrees the lusts of the flesh, until it removed entirely the inclination for sexual intercourse engendered by habit. For presently one is introduced earnestly deprecating, from henceforth, this seduction, saying, "O Lord, Father, and Governor of my life, leave me not to their counsels; give me not a proud look; let not the greediness of the belly, nor lust of the flesh, take hold of me." And in the Book of Wisdom, a book full of all virtue, the Holy Spirit, now openly drawing His hearers to continence and chastity, sings on this wise, "Better it is to have no children, and to have virtue, for the memorial thereof is immortal; because it is known with God and with men. When it is present men take example at it; and when it is gone they desire it: it wears a crown and triumphed forever, having gotten the victory, striving for undefiled rewards."

Chapter IV.—Christ Alone Taught Virginity, Openly Preaching the Kingdom of Heaven; The Likeness of God to Be Attained in the Light of the Divine Virtues.

We have already spoken of the periods of the human race, and how, beginning with the intermarriage of brothers and sisters, it went on to continence; and we have now left for us the subject of virginity. Let us then endeavor to speak of this as well as we can. And first let us inquire for what reason it was that no one of the many patriarchs and prophets and righteous men, who taught and did many noble things, either praised or chose the state of virginity. Because it was reserved for the Lord alone to be the first to teach this doctrine, since He alone, coming down to us, taught man to draw near to God; for it was fitting that He who was first and chief of priests, of prophets, and of angels, should also be saluted as first and chief of virgins. For in old times man was not yet perfect, and for this reason was unable to receive perfection, which is virginity. For, being made in the *Image* of God, he needed to receive that which was according to His *Likeness*; which the Word being sent down into the world to perfect, He first took upon Him our form, disfigured as it was by many sins, in order that we, for whose sake He bore it, might be able again to receive the divine *form*. For it is then that we are truly fashioned in the likeness of God, when we represent His features in a human life, like skillful painters, stamping them upon ourselves as upon tablets, learning the path which He showed us. And for this reason He, being God, was pleased to put on human flesh, so that we, beholding as on a tablet the divine Pattern of our life, should also be able to imitate Him who painted it. For He was not one who, thinking one thing, did another; nor, while He considered one thing to be right, taught another. But whatever things were truly useful and right, these He both taught and did.

Chapter V.—Christ, by Preserving His Flesh Incorrupt in Virginity, Draws to the Exercise of Virginity; The Small Number of Virgins in Proportion to the Number of Saints.

What then did the Lord, who is the Truth and the Light, take in hand when He came down from heaven? He preserved the flesh which He had taken upon Him incorrupt in virginity, so that we also, if we would come to the likeness of God and Christ, should endeavor to honor virginity. For the likeness of God is the avoiding of corruption. And that the Word, when He was incarnate, became chief Virgin, in the same way as He was chief Shepherd and chief Prophet of the Church, the Christ-possessed John shows us, saying, in the Book of the Revelation, "And I looked, and, lo, a Lamb stood on the mount Sion, and with Him an hundred forty and four thousand, having His name and His Father's name written in their foreheads. And I heard a voice from heaven, as the voice of many waters, and as the voice of a great thunder; and I heard the voice of harpers harping with their harps: And they sung as it were a new song before the throne, and before the four beasts, and the elders: and no man could learn that song but the hundred and forty and four thousand, which were redeemed from the earth. These are they which were not defiled with women; for they are virgins. These are they who follow the Lamb whithersoever He goes;" showing that the Lord is leader of the choir of virgins. And remark, in addition to this, how very great in the sight of God is the dignity of virginity: "These were redeemed from among men, being the first-fruits unto God and to the Lamb. And in their mouth was found no guile: for they are without fault," he says, "and they follow the Lamb whithersoever He goes." And he clearly intends by this to teach us that the number of virgins was, from the beginning, restricted to so many, namely, a hundred and forty and four thousand, while the multitude of the other saints is innumerable. For let us consider what he means when discoursing of the rest. "I beheld a great multitude, which no man could number, of all nations, and kindred, and people, and tongues." It is plain, therefore, as I said, that in the case of the other saints he introduces an unspeakable multitude, while in the case of those who are in a state of virginity he mentions only a very small number, so as to make a strong contrast with those who make up the innumerable number.

This, O Arete, is my discourse to you on the subject of virginity. But, if I have omitted anything, let Theophila, who succeeds me, supply the omission.

Discourse II.—Theophila.

Chapter I.—Marriage Not Abolished by the Commendation of Virginity.

And then, she said, Theophila spoke:—Since Marcella has excellently begun this discussion without sufficiently completing it, it is necessary that I should endeavor to put a finish to it. Now, the fact that man has advanced by degrees to virginity, God urging him on from time to time, seems to me to have been admirably proved; but I cannot say the same *as to the assertion* that from henceforth they should no longer beget children. For I think I have perceived clearly from the Scriptures that, after He had brought in virginity, the Word did not altogether abolish the generation of children; for although the moon may be greater than the stars, the light of the other stars is not destroyed by the moonlight.

Let us begin with Genesis, that we may give its place of antiquity and supremacy to this scripture. Now the sentence and ordinance of God respecting the begetting of children is confessedly being fulfilled to this day, the Creator still fashioning man. For this is quite manifest, that God, like a painter, is at this very time working at the world, as the Lord also taught, "My Father works hitherto." But when the rivers shall cease to flow and fall into the reservoir of the sea, and the light shall be perfectly separated from the darkness,—for the separation is still going on,—and the dry land shall henceforth cease to bring forth its fruits with creeping things and four-footed beasts, and the predestined number of men shall be fulfilled; then from henceforth shall men abstain from the generation of children. But at present man must cooperate in the forming of the image of God, while the world exists and is still being formed; for it is said, "Increase and multiply." And we must not be offended at the ordinance of the Creator, from which, moreover, we ourselves have our being. For the casting of seed into the furrows of the matrix is the beginning of the generation of men, so that bone taken from bone, and flesh from flesh, by an invisible power, are fashioned into another man. And in this way we must consider that the saying is fulfilled, "This is now bone of my bone, and flesh of my flesh."

Chapter II.—Generation Something Akin to the First Formation of Eve from the Side and Nature of Adam; God the Creator of Men in Ordinary Generation.

And this perhaps is what was shadowed forth by the sleep and trance of the first man, which prefigured the embraces of connubial love. When thirsting for children a man falls into a kind of trance, softened and subdued by the pleasures of generation as by sleep, so that again something drawn from his flesh and from his bones is, as I said, fashioned into another man. For the harmony of the bodies being disturbed in the embraces of love, as those tell us who have experience of the marriage state, all the marrow-like and generative part of the blood, like a kind of liquid bone, coming together from all the members, worked into foam and curdled, is projected through the organs of generation into the living body of the female. And probably it is for this reason that a man is said to leave his father and his mother, since he is then suddenly unmindful of all things when united to his wife in the embraces of love, he is overcome by the desire of generation, offering his side to the divine Creator to take away from it, so that the father may again appear in the son.

Wherefore, if God still forms man, shall we not be guilty of audacity if we think of the generation of children as something offensive, which the Almighty Himself is not ashamed to make use of in working with His undefiled hands; for He says to Jeremiah, "Before I formed thee in the belly I knew thee;" and to Job, "Didst thou take clay and form a living creature, and make it speak upon the earth?" and Job draws near to Him in supplication, saying, "Thine hands have made me and fashioned me." Would it not, then, be absurd to forbid marriage unions, seeing that we expect that after us there will be martyrs, and those who shall oppose the evil one, for whose sake also the Word promised that He would shorten those days? For if the generation of children henceforth had seemed evil to God, as you said, for what reason will those who have come into existence in opposition to the divine decree and will be able to appear well-pleasing to God? And must not that which is begotten be something spurious, and not a creature of God, if, like a counterfeit coin, it is molded apart from the intention and ordinance of the lawful authority? And so we concede to men the power of forming men.

Chapter III.—An Ambiguous Passage of Scripture; Not Only the Faithful But Even Prelates Sometimes Illegitimate.

But Marcella, interrupting, said, "O Theophila, there appears here a great mistake, and something contrary to what you have said; and do you think to escape under cover of the cloud which you have thrown around you? For there comes that argument, which perhaps anyone who addresses you as a very wise person will bring forward: What do you say of those who are begotten unlawfully in adultery? For you laid it down that it was inconceivable and impossible for anyone to enter into the world unless he was introduced by the will of the divine Ruler, his frame being prepared for him by God. And that you may not take refuge behind a safe wall, bringing forward the Scripture which says, 'As for the children of the adulterers, they shall not come to their perfection,' he will answer you easily, that we often see those who are unlawfully begotten coming to perfection like ripe fruit.

And if, again, you answer sophistically, 'O, my friend, by those who come not to perfection I understand being perfected in Christ-taught righteousness;' he will say, 'But, indeed, my worthy friend, very many who are begotten of unrighteous seed are not only numbered among those who are gathered into the flock of the brethren, but are often called even to preside over them. Since, then, it is clear, and all testify, that those who are born of adultery do come to perfection, we must not imagine that the Spirit was teaching respecting conceptions and births, but rather perhaps concerning those who adulterate the truth, who, corrupting the Scriptures by false doctrines, bring forth an imperfect and immature wisdom, mixing their error with piety.' And, therefore, this plea being taken away from you, come now and tell us if those who are born of adultery are begotten by the will of God; for you said that it was impossible that the offspring of a man should be brought to perfection unless the Lord formed it and gave it life."

Chapter IV.—Human Generation, and the Work of God Therein Set Forth.

Theophila, as though caught round the middle by a strong antagonist, grew giddy, and with difficulty recovering herself, replied, "You ask a question, my worthy friend, which needs to be solved by an example, that you may still better understand how the creative power of God, pervading all things, is more especially the real cause in the generation of men, making those things to grow which are planted in the productive earth. For that which is sown is not to be blamed, but he who sows in a strange soil by unlawful embraces, as though purchasing a slight pleasure by shamefully selling his own seed. For imagine our birth into the world to be like some such thing as a house having its entrance lying close to lofty mountains; and that the house extends a great way down, far from the entrance, and that it has many holes behind, and that in this part it has circular." "I imagine it," said Marcella. "Well, then, suppose that a modeler seated within is fashioning many statues; imagine, again, that the substance of clay is incessantly brought to him from without, through the holes, by many men who do not any of them see the artist himself. Now suppose the house to be covered with mist and clouds, and nothing visible to those who are outside but only the holes." "Let this also be supposed," she said. "And that each one of those who are laboring together to provide the clay has one hole allotted to himself, into which he alone has to bring and deposit his own clay, not touching any other hole. And if, again, he shall officiously endeavor to open that which is allotted to another, let him be threatened with fire and scourges.

"Well, now, consider further what comes after this: the modeler within going round to the holes and taking privately for his modelling the clay which he finds at each hole, and having in a certain number of months made his model, giving it back through the same hole; having this for his rule, that every lump of clay which is capable of being molded shall be worked up indifferently, even if it be unlawfully thrown by anyone through another's hole, for the clay has done no wrong, and, therefore, as being blameless, should be molded and formed; but that he who, in opposition to the ordinance and law, deposited it in another's hole, should be punished as a criminal and transgressor. For the clay should not be blamed, but he who did this in violation of what is right; for, through incontinence, having carried it away, he secretly, by violence, deposited it in another's hole." "You say most truly."

Chapter V.—The Holy Father Follows Up the Same Argument.

And now that these things are completed, it remains for you to apply this picture, my wisest of friends, to the things which have been already spoken of; comparing the house to the invisible nature of our generation, and the entrance adjacent to the mountains to the sending down of our souls from heaven, and their descent into the bodies; the holes to the female sex, and the modeler to the creative power of God, which, under the cover of generation, making use of our nature, invisibly forms us men within, working the garments for the souls. Those who carry the clay represent the male sex in the comparison; when thirsting for children, they bring and cast in seed into the natural channels of the female, as those in the comparison cast clay into the holes. For the seed, which, so to speak, partakes of a divine creative power, is not to be thought guilty of the incentives to incontinence; and art always works up the matter submitted to it; and nothing is to be considered as evil in itself, but becomes so by the act of those who used it in such a way; for when properly and purely made use of, it comes out pure, but if disgracefully and improperly, then it becomes disgraceful. For how did iron, which was discovered for the benefit of agriculture and the arts, injure those who sharpened it for murderous battles? Or how did gold, or silver, or brass, and, to take it collectively, the whole of the workable earth, injure those who, ungratefully towards their Creator, make a wrong use of them by turning parts of them into various kinds of idols? And if anyone should supply wool from that which had been stolen to the weaving art, that art, regarding this one thing only, manufactures the material submitted to it, if it will receive the preparation, rejecting nothing of that which is serviceable to itself, since that which is stolen is here not to be blamed, being lifeless. And, therefore, the material itself is to be wrought and adorned, but he who is discovered to have abstracted it unjustly should be punished. So, in like manner, the violators of marriage, and those who break the strings of the harmony of life, as of a harp, raging with lust, and letting loose their desires in adultery, should themselves be tortured and punished, for they do a great wrong stealing from the gardens of others the embraces of generation; but the seed itself, as in the case of the wool, should be formed and endowed with life.

Chapter VI.—God Cares Even for Adulterous Births; Angels Given to Them as Guardians.

But what need is there to protract the argument by using such examples? For nature could not thus, in a little time, accomplish so great a work without divine help. For who gave to the bones their fixed nature? And who bound the yielding members with nerves, to be extended and relaxed at the joints? Or who prepared channels for the blood, and a soft windpipe for the breath? Or what god caused the humors to ferment, mixing them with blood and forming the soft flesh out of the earth, but only the Supreme Artist making us to be man, the rational and living image of Himself, and forming it like wax, in the womb, from moist slight seed? Or by whose providence was it that the fetus was not suffocated by damp when shut up within, in the connexion of the vessels? Or who, after it was brought forth and had come into the light, changed it from weakness and smallness to size, and beauty, and strength, unless God Himself, the Supreme Artist, as I said, making by His creative power copies of Christ, and living pictures? Whence, also, we have received from the inspired writings, that those who are begotten, even though it be in adultery, are committed to guardian angels. But if they came into being in opposition to the will and the decree of the blessed nature of God, how should they be delivered over to angels, to be nourished with much gentleness and indulgence? and how, if they had to accuse their own parents, could they confidently, before the judgment seat of Christ, invoke Him and say, "Thou didst not, O Lord, grudge us this common light; but these appointed us to death, despising Thy command?" "For," He says, "children begotten of unlawful beds are witnesses of wickedness against their parents at their trial."

Chapter VII.—The Rational Soul from God Himself; Chastity Not the Only Good, Although the Best and Most Honored.

And perhaps there will be room for some to argue plausibly among those who are wanting in discrimination and judgment, that this fleshly garment of the soul, being planted by men, is shaped spontaneously apart from the sentence of God. If, however, he should teach that the immortal being of the soul also is sown along with the mortal body, he will not be believed; for the Almighty alone breathes into man the undying and undecaying part, as also it is He alone who is Creator of the invisible and indestructible. For, He says, He "breathed into his nostrils the breath of life; and man became a living soul." And those artificers who, to the destruction of men, make images in human form, not perceiving and knowing their own Maker, are blamed by the Word, which says, in the Book of Wisdom, a book full of all virtue, "his heart is ashes, his hope is more vile than earth, and his life of less value than clay; forasmuch as he knew not his Maker, and Him that inspired into him an active soul, and breathed in a living spirit;" that is, God, the Maker of all men; therefore, also, according to the apostle, He "will have all men to be saved, and to come unto the knowledge of the truth." And now, although this subject be scarcely completed, yet there are others which remain to be discussed. For when one thoroughly examines and understands those things which happen to man according to his nature, he will know not to despise the procreation of children, although he applauds chastity, and prefers it in honor. For although honey be sweeter and more pleasant than other things, we are not for that reason to consider other things bitter which are mixed up in the natural sweetness of fruits. And, in support of these statements, I will bring forward a trustworthy witness, namely, Paul, who says, "So then he that giveth her in marriage doeth well; but he that giveth her not in marriage doeth better." Now the word, in setting forth that which is better and sweeter, did not intend to take away the inferior, but arranges so as to assign to each its own proper use and advantage. For there are some to whom it is not given to attain virginity; and there are others whom He no longer wills to be excited by procreations to lust, and to be defiled, but henceforth to meditate and to keep the mind upon the transformation of the body to the likeness of angels, when they "neither marry nor are given in marriage," according to the infallible words of the Lord; since it is not given to all to attain that undefiled state of being a eunuch for the sake of the kingdom of heaven, but manifestly to those only who are able to preserve the ever-blooming and unfading flower of virginity. For it is the custom of the prophetic Word to compare the Church to a flower covered and variegated meadow, adorned and crowned not only with the flowers of virginity, but also with those of child-bearing and of continence; for it is written, "Upon thy right hand did stand the queen in a vesture of gold, wrought about with divers colors."

These words, O Arete, I bring according to my ability to this discussion in behalf of the truth.

And when Theophila had thus spoken, Theopatra said that applause arose from all the virgins approving of her discourse; and that when they became silent, after a long pause, Thaleia arose, for to her had been assigned the third place in the contest, that which came after Theophila. And she then, as I think, followed, and spoke.

Discourse III.—Thaleia.
Chapter I.—Passages of Holy Scripture Compared.

You seem to me, O Theophila, to excel all in action and in speech, and to be second to none in wisdom. For there is no one who will find fault with your discourse, however contentious and contradictory he may be. Yet, while everything else seems rightly spoken, one thing, my friend, distresses and troubles me, considering that that wise and most spiritual man—I mean Paul—would not vainly refer to Christ and the Church the union of the first man and woman, if the Scripture meant nothing higher than what is conveyed by the mere words and the history; for if we are to take the Scripture as a bare representation wholly referring to the union of man and woman, for what reason should the apostle, calling these things to remembrance, and guiding us, as I opine, into the way of the Spirit, allegorize the history of Adam and Eve as having a reference to Christ and the Church? For the passage in Genesis reads thus: "And Adam said, This is now bone of my bones, and flesh of my flesh: she shall be called Woman, because she was taken out of man. Therefore shall a man leave his father and his mother, and shall cleave unto his wife: and they shall be one flesh." But the apostle considering this passage, by no means, as I said, intends to take it according to its mere natural sense, as referring to the union of man and woman, as you do; for you, explaining the passage in too natural a sense, laid down that the Spirit is speaking only of conception and births; that the bone taken from the bones was made another man, and that living creatures coming together swell like trees at the time of conception. But he, more spiritually referring the passage to Christ, thus teaches: "He that loves his wife loves himself. For no man ever yet hated his own flesh, but nourishes and cherishes it, even as the Lord the Church: for we are members of His body, of His flesh, and of His bones. For this cause shall a man leave his father and mother, and shall be joined unto his wife, and they two shall be one flesh. This is a great mystery: but I speak concerning Christ and the Church."

Chapter II.—The Digressions of the Apostle Paul; The Character of His Doctrine: Nothing in It Contradictory; Condemnation of Origen, Who Wrongly Turns Everything into Allegory.

Let it not disturb you, if, in discussing one class of subjects, he, i.e., *Paul*, should pass over into another, so as to appear to mix them up, and to import matters foreign to the subject under consideration, departing from the question, as now for instance. For wishing, as it seems, to strengthen most carefully the argument on behalf of chastity, he prepares the mode of argument beforehand, beginning with the more persuasive mode of speech. For the character of his speech being very various, and arranged for the purpose of progressive proof, begins gently, but flows forward into a style which is loftier and more magnificent. And then, again changing to what is deep, he sometimes finishes with what is simple and easy, and sometimes with what is more difficult and delicate; and yet introducing nothing which is foreign to the subject by these changes, but, bringing them all together according to a certain marvelous relationship, he works into one the question which is set forth as his subject. It is needful, then, that I should more accurately unfold the meaning of the apostle's arguments, yet rejecting nothing of what has been said before. For you seem to me, O Theophila, to have discussed those words of the Scripture amply and clearly, and to have set them forth as they are without mistake. For it is a dangerous thing wholly to despise the literal meaning, as has been said, and especially of Genesis, where the unchangeable decrees of God for the constitution of the universe are set forth, in agreement with which, even until now, the world is perfectly ordered, most beautifully in accordance with a perfect rule, until the Lawgiver Himself having re-arranged it, wishing to order it anew, shall break up the first laws of nature by a fresh disposition. But, since it is not fitting to leave the demonstration of the argument unexamined—and, so to speak, half-lame—come let us, as it were completing our pair, bring forth the analogical sense, looking more deeply into the Scripture; for Paul is not to be despised when he passes over the literal meaning, and shows that the words extend to Christ and the Church.

Chapter III.—Comparison Instituted Between the First and Second Adam.

And, first, we must inquire if Adam can be likened to the Son of God, when he was found in the transgression of the Fall, and heard the sentence, "Dust thou art, and unto dust shalt thou return." For how shall he be considered "the first-born of every creature," who, after the creation of the earth and the firmament, was formed out of clay? And how shall he be admitted to be "the tree of life" who was cast out for his transgression, lest "he should again stretch forth his hand and eat of it, and live forever?" For it is necessary that a thing which is likened unto anything else, should in many respects be similar and analogous to that of which it is the similitude, and not have its constitution opposite and dissimilar. For one who should venture to compare the uneven to the even, or harmony to discord, would not be considered rational. But the even should be compared to that which in its nature is even, although it should be even only in a small measure; and the white to that which in its nature is white, even although it should be very small, and should show but moderately the whiteness by reason of which it is called white. Now, it is beyond all doubt clear to everyone, that that which is sinless and incorrupt is even, and harmonious, and bright as wisdom; but that that which is mortal and sinful is uneven and discordant, and cast out as guilty and subject to condemnation.

Chapter IV.—Some Things Here Hard and Too Slightly Treated, and Apparently Not Sufficiently Brought Out According to the Rule of Theology.

Such, then, I consider to be the objections urged by many who, despising, as it seems, the wisdom of Paul, dislike the comparing of the first man to Christ. For come, let us consider how rightly Paul compared Adam to Christ, not only considering him to be the type and image, but also that Christ Himself became the very same thing, because the Eternal Word fell upon Him. For it was fitting that the first-born of God, the first shoot, the only begotten, even the wisdom of God, should be joined to the first-formed man, and first and first-born of mankind, and should become incarnate. And this was Christ, a man filled with the pure and perfect Godhead, and God received into man. For it was most suitable that the oldest of the Æons and the first of the Archangels, when about to hold communion with men, should dwell in the oldest and the first of men, even Adam. And thus, when renovating those things which were from the beginning, and forming them again of the Virgin by the Spirit, He frames the same just as at the beginning. When the earth was still virgin and untilled, God, taking mold, formed the reasonable creature from it without seed.

Chapter V.—A Passage of Jeremiah Examined.

And here I may adduce the prophet Jeremiah as a trustworthy and lucid witness, who speaks thus: "Then I went down to the potter's house; and, behold, he wrought a work on the wheels. And the vessel that he made of clay was marred in the hand of the potter: so he made it again another vessel, as seemed good to the potter to make it." For when Adam, having been formed out of clay, was still soft and moist, and not yet, like a tile, made hard and incorruptible, sin ruined him, flowing and dropping down upon him like water. And therefore God, moistening him afresh and forming anew the same clay to His honor, having first hardened and fixed it in the Virgin's womb, and united and mixed it with the Word, brought it forth into life no longer soft and broken; lest, being overflowed again by streams of corruption from without, it should become soft, and perish as the Lord in His teaching shows in the parable of the finding of the sheep; where my Lord says to those standing by, "What man of you, having an hundred sheep, if he lose one of them, doth not leave the ninety and nine in the wilderness, and go after that which is lost until he find it? And when he hath found it, he lays it on his shoulders rejoicing; and when he comes home, he calls together his friends and neighbors, saying unto them, Rejoice with me; for I have found my sheep which was lost."

Chapter VI.—The Whole Number of Spiritual Sheep; Man a Second Choir, After the Angels, to the Praise of God; The Parable of the Lost Sheep Explained.

Now, since He truly was and is, being in the beginning with God, and being God, He is the chief Commander and Shepherd of the heavenly ones, whom all reasonable creatures obey and attend, who tends in order and numbers the multitudes of the blessed angels. For this is the equal and perfect number of immortal creatures, divided according to their races and tribes, man also being here taken into the flock. For he also was created without corruption, that he might honor the king and maker of all things, responding to the shouts of the melodious angels which came from heaven. But when it came to pass that, by transgressing the commandment (of God), he suffered a terrible and destructive fall, being thus reduced to a state of death, for this reason the Lord says that He came from heaven into (a human) life, leaving the ranks and the armies of angels. For the mountains are to be explained by the heavens, and the ninety and nine sheep by the principalities and powers which the Captain and Shepherd left when He went down to seek the lost one. For it remained that man should be included in this catalogue and number, the Lord lifting him up and wrapping him round, that he might not again, as I said, be overflowed and swallowed up by the waves of deceit. For with this purpose the Word assumed the nature of man, that, having overcome the serpent, He might by Himself destroy the condemnation which had come into being along with man's ruin. For it was fitting that the Evil One should be overcome by no other, but by him whom he had deceived, and whom he was boasting that he held in subjection, because no otherwise was it possible that sin and condemnation should be destroyed, unless that same man on whose account it had been said, "Dust thou art, and unto dust thou shalt return," should be created anew, and undo the sentence which for his sake had gone forth on all, that "as in Adam" at first "all die, even so" again "in Christ," who assumed the *nature and position of* Adam, should "all be made alive."

Chapter VII.—The Works of Christ, Proper to God and to Man, the Works of Him Who is One.

And now we seem to have said almost enough on the fact that man has become the organ and clothing of the Only-begotten, and what He was who came to dwell in him. But the fact that there is no *moral* inequality or discord may again be considered briefly from the beginning. For he speaks well who says that that is in its own nature good and righteous and holy, by participation of which other things become good, and that wisdom is in connection with God, and that, on the other hand, sin is unholy and unrighteous and evil. For life and death, corruption and incorruption, are two things in the highest degree opposed to each other. For life is a *moral* equality, but corruption an inequality; and righteousness and prudence a harmony, but unrighteousness and folly a discord. Now, man being between these is neither righteousness itself, nor unrighteousness; but being placed midway between incorruption and corruption, to whichever of these he may incline is said to partake of the nature of that which has laid hold of him. Now, when he inclines to corruption, he becomes corrupt and mortal, and when to incorruption, he becomes incorrupt and immortal. For, being placed midway between the tree of life and the tree of the knowledge of good and evil, of the Fruit of which he tasted, he was changed into the nature of the latter, himself being neither the tree of life nor that of corruption; but having been shown forth as mortal, from his participation in and presence with corruption, and, again, as incorrupt and immortal by connection with and participation in life; as Paul also taught, saying, "Corruption shall not inherit incorruption, nor death life," rightly defining corruption and death to be that which corrupts and kills, and not that which is corrupted and dies; and incorruption and life that which gives life and immortality, and not that which receives life and immortality. And thus man is neither a discord and an inequality, nor an equality and a harmony. But when he received discord, which is transgression and sin, he became discordant and unseemly; but when he received harmony, that is righteousness, he became a harmonious and seemly organ, in order that the Lord, the Incorruption which conquered death, might harmonize the resurrection with the flesh, not suffering it again to be inherited by corruption. And on this point also let these statements suffice.

Chapter VIII.—The Bones and Flesh of Wisdom; The Side Out of Which the Spiritual Eve is Formed, the Holy Spirit; The Woman the Help-Meet of Adam; Virgins Betrothed to Christ.

For it has been already established by no contemptible arguments from Scripture, that the first man may be properly referred to Christ Himself, and is no longer a type and representation and image of the Only-begotten, but has become actually Wisdom and the Word.

For man, having been composed, like water, of wisdom and life, has become identical with the very same untainted light which poured into him. Whence it was that the apostle directly referred to Christ the words which had been spoken of Adam. For thus will it be most certainly agreed that the Church is formed out of His bones and flesh; and it was for this cause that the Word, leaving His Father in heaven, came down to be "joined to His wife;" and slept in the trance of His passion, and willingly suffered death for her, that He might present the Church to Himself glorious and blameless, having cleansed her by the laver, for the receiving of the spiritual and blessed seed, which is sown by Him who with whispers implants it in the depths of the mind; and is conceived and formed by the Church, as by a woman. so as to give birth and nourishment to virtue. For in this way, too, the command, "Increase and multiply," is duly fulfilled, the Church increasing daily in greatness and beauty and multitude, by the union and communion of the Word who now still comes down to us and falls into a trance by the memorial of His passion; for otherwise the Church could not conceive believers, and give them new birth by the laver of regeneration, unless Christ, emptying Himself for their sake, that He might be contained by them, as I said, through the recapitulation of His passion, should die again, coming down from heaven, and being "joined to His wife," the Church, should provide for a certain power being taken from His own side, so that all who are built up in Him should grow up, even those who are born again by the laver, receiving of His bones and of His flesh, that is, of His holiness and of His glory. For he who says that the bones and flesh of Wisdom are understanding and virtue, says most rightly; and that the side is the Spirit of truth, the Paraclete, of whom the illuminated receiving are fitly born again to incorruption. For it is impossible for anyone to be a partaker of the Holy Spirit, and to be chosen a member of Christ, unless the Word first came down upon him and fell into a trance, in order that he, being filled with the Spirit, and rising again from sleep with Him who was laid to sleep for his sake, should be able to receive renewal and restoration. For He may fitly be called the side of the Word, even the sevenfold Spirit of truth, according to the prophet; of whom God taking, in the trance of Christ, that is, after His incarnation and passion, prepares a helpmeet for Him—I mean the souls which are betrothed and given in marriage to Him. For it is frequently the case that the Scriptures thus call the assembly and mass of believers by the name of the Church, the more perfect in their progress being led up to be the one person and body of the Church. For those who are the better, and who embrace the truth more clearly, being delivered from the evils of the flesh, become, on account of their perfect purification and faith, a church and help-meet of Christ, betrothed and given in marriage to Him as a virgin, according to the apostle, so that receiving the pure and genuine seed of His doctrine, they may co-operate with Him, helping in preaching for the salvation of others. And those who are still imperfect and beginning their lessons, are born to salvation, and shaped, as by mothers, by those who are more perfect, until they are brought forth and regenerated unto the greatness and beauty of virtue; and so these, in their turn making progress, having become a church, assist in laboring for the birth and nurture of other children, accomplishing in the receptacle of the soul, as in a womb, the blameless will of the Word.

Chapter IX.—The Dispensation of Grace in Paul the Apostle.

Now we should consider the case of the renowned Paul, that when he was not yet perfect in Christ, he was first born and suckled, Ananias preaching to him, and renewing him in baptism, as the history in the Acts relates. But when he was grown to a man, and was built up, then being molded to spiritual perfection, he was made the help-meet and bride of the Word; and receiving and conceiving the seeds of life, he who was before a child, becomes a church and a mother, himself laboring in birth of those who, through him, believed in the Lord, until Christ was formed and born in them also. For he says, "My little children, of whom I travail in birth again until Christ be formed in you;" and again, "In Christ Jesus I have begotten you through the Gospel."

It is evident, then, that the statement respecting Eve and Adam is to be referred to the Church and Christ. For this is truly a great mystery and a supernatural, of which I, from my weakness and dullness, am unable to speak, according to its worth and greatness. Nevertheless, let us attempt it. It remains that I speak to you on what follows, and of its signification.

Chapter X.—The Doctrine of the Same Apostle Concerning Purity.

Now Paul, when summoning all persons to sanctification and purity, in this way referred that which had been spoken concerning the first man and Eve in a secondary sense to Christ and the Church, in order to silence the ignorant, now deprived of all excuse. For men who are incontinent in consequence of the uncontrolled impulses of sensuality in them, dare to force the Scriptures beyond their true meaning, so as to twist into a defense of their incontinence the saying, "Increase and multiply;" and the other, "Therefore shall a man leave his father and his mother;" and they are not ashamed to run counter to the Spirit, but, as though born for this purpose, they kindle up the shouldering and lurking passion, fanning and provoking it; and therefore he, cutting off very sharply these dishonest follies and invented excuses, and having arrived at the subject of instructing them how men should behave to their wives, showing that it should be as Christ did to the Church, "who gave Himself for it, that He might sanctify and cleanse it by the washing of water by the Word," he referred back to Genesis, mentioning the things spoken concerning the first man, and explaining these things as bearing on the subject before him, that he might take away occasion for the abuse of these passages from those who taught the sensual gratification of the body, under the pretext of begetting children.

Chapter XI.—The Same Argument.

For consider, O virgins, how he, desiring with all his might that believers in Christ should be chaste, endeavors by many arguments to show them the dignity of chastity, as when he says, Now, concerning the things whereof ye wrote unto me: It is good for a man not to touch a woman," thence showing already very clearly that it is good not to touch a woman, laying it down. and setting it forth unconditionally. But afterwards, being aware of the weakness of the less continent, and their passion for intercourse, he permitted those who are unable to govern the flesh to use their own wives, rather than, shamefully transgressing, to give themselves up to fornication. Then, after having given this permission, he immediately added these words, "that Satan tempt you not for your incontinency;" which means, "if you, such as you are, cannot, on account of the incontinence and softness of your bodies, be perfectly continent, I will rather permit you to have intercourse with your own wives, lest, professing perfect continence, ye be constantly tempted by the evil one, and be inflamed with lust after other men's wives."

Chapter XII.—Paul an Example to Widows, and to Those Who Do Not Live with Their Wives.

Come, now, and let us examine more carefully the very words which are before us, and observe that the apostle did not grant these things unconditionally to all, but first laid down the reason on account of which he was led to this. For, having set forth that "it is good for a man not to touch a woman," he added immediately, "Nevertheless, to avoid fornication, let every man have his own wife"—that is, "on account of the fornication which would arise from your being unable to restrain your voluptuousness"—"and let every woman have her own husband. Let the husband render unto the wife due benevolence: and likewise also the wife unto the husband. The wife hath not power of her own body, but the husband: and likewise also the husband hath not power of his own body, but the wife. Defraud ye not one the other, except it be with consent for a time, that ye may give yourselves to prayer; and come together again, that Satan tempt you not for your incontinency. But I speak this by permission, and not of commandment." And this is very carefully considered. "By permission" he says, showing that he was giving counsel, "not of command;" for he receives *command* respecting chastity and the not touching of a woman, but *permission* respecting those who are unable, as I said, to chasten their appetites. These things, then, he lays down concerning men and women who are married to one spouse, or who shall hereafter be so; but we must now examine carefully the apostle's language respecting men who have lost their wives, and women who have lost their husbands, and what he declares on this subject.

"I say therefore," he goes on, "to the unmarried and widows, It is good for them if they abide even as I. But if they cannot contain, let them marry: for it is better to marry than to burn." Here also he persisted in giving the preference to continence. For, taking himself as a notable example, in order to stir them up to emulation, he challenged his hearers to this state of life, teaching that it was better that a man who had been bound to one wife should henceforth remain single, as he also did. But if, on the other hand, this should be a matter of difficulty to anyone, on account of the strength of animal passion, he allows that one who is in such a condition may, "by permission," contract a second marriage; not as though he expressed the opinion that a second marriage was in itself good, but judging it better than burning. Just as though, in the fast which prepares for the Easter celebration, one should offer food to another who was dangerously ill, and say," In truth, my friend, it were fitting and good that you should bravely hold out like us, and partake of the same things, for it is forbidden even to think of food to-day; but since you are held down and weakened by disease, and cannot bear it, therefore, 'by permission,' we advise you to eat food, lest, being quite unable, from sickness, to hold up against the desire for food, you perish." Thus also the apostle speaks here, first saying that he wished all were healthy and continent, as he also was, but afterwards allowing a second marriage to those who are burdened with the disease of the passions, lest they should be wholly defiled by fornication, goaded on by the itchings of the organs of generation to promiscuous intercourse, considering such a second marriage far preferable to burning and indecency.

Chapter XIII.—The Doctrine of Paul Concerning Virginity Explained.

I have now brought to an end what I have to say respecting continence and marriage and chastity, and intercourse with men, and in which of these there is help towards progress in righteousness; but it still remains to speak concerning virginity—if, indeed, anything be prescribed on this subject. Let us then treat this subject also; for it stands thus: "Now concerning virgins, I have no commandment of the Lord: yet I give my judgment, as one that hath obtained mercy of the Lord to be faithful. I suppose therefore that this is good for the present distress; I say, that it is good for a man so to be. Art thou bound unto a wife? Seek not to be loosed. Art thou loosed from a wife? Seek not a wife. But and if thou marry, thou hast not sinned; and if a virgin marry, she has not sinned. Nevertheless such shall have trouble in the flesh: but I spare you." Having given his opinion with great caution respecting virginity, and being about to advise him who wished it to give his virgin in marriage, so that none of those things which conduce to sanctification should be of necessity and by compulsion, but according to the free purpose of the soul. for this is acceptable to God, he does not wish these things to be said as by authority, and as the mind of the Lord, with reference to the giving of a virgin in marriage; for after he had said, "if a virgin marry, she hath not sinned," directly afterwards, with the greatest caution, he modified his statement, showing that he had advised these things by human permission, and not by divine. So, immediately after he had said, "if a virgin marry, she hath not sinned," he added, "such shall have trouble in the flesh: but I spare you." By which he means: "I sparing you, such as you are, consented to these things, because you have chosen to think thus of them, that I may not seem to hurry you on by violence, and compel anyone to this. But yet if it shall please you who find chastity hard to bear, rather to turn to marriage; I consider it to be profitable for you to restrain yourselves in the gratification of the flesh, not making your marriage an occasion for abusing your own vessels to uncleanness." Then he adds, "But this I say, brethren, the time is short: it remained, that both they that have wives be as though they had none." And again, going on and challenging them to the same things, he confirmed his statement, powerfully supporting the state of virginity, and adding expressly the following words to those which he had spoken before, he exclaimed, "I would have you without carefulness. He that is unmarried cares for the things that belong to the Lord: but he that is married cares for the things that are of the world, how he may please his wife. There is a difference also between a wife and a virgin. The unmarried woman cares for the things of the Lord, that she may be holy both in body and in spirit: but she that is married cares for the things of the world, how she may please her husband." Now it is clear to all, without any doubt, that to care for the things of the Lord and to please God, is much better than to care for the things of the world and to please one's wife. For who is there so foolish and blind. As not to perceive in this statement the higher praise which Paul accords to chastity? "And this," he says, "I speak for your own profit, not that I may cast a snare upon you, but for that which is comely."

Chapter XIV.—Virginity a Gift of God: the Purpose of Virginity Not Rashly to Be Adopted by Any One.

Consider besides how, in addition to the words already quoted, he commends the state of virginity as a gift of God. Wherefore he rejects those of the more incontinent, who, under the influence of vain-glory, would advance to this state, advising them to marry, lest in their time of manly strength, the flesh stirring up the desires and passions, they should be goaded on to defile the soul. For let us consider what he lays down: "But if any man think that he behaves himself uncomely towards his virgin," he says," if she pass the flower of her age, and need so require, let him do what he will, he sinned not: let him marry;" properly here preferring marriage to "uncomeliness," in the case of those who had chosen the state of virginity, but afterwards finding it intolerable and grievous, and in word boasting of their perseverance before men, out of shame, but indeed no longer having the power to persevere in the life of a eunuch. But for him who of his own free will and purpose decides to preserve his flesh in virgin purity, "having no necessity," that is, passion calling forth his loins to intercourse, for there are, as it seems, differences in men's bodies; such a one contending and struggling, and zealously abiding by his profession, and admirably fulfilling it, he exhorts to abide and to preserve it, according the highest prize to virginity. For he that is able, he says, and ambitious to preserve his flesh pure, does better; but he that is unable, and enters into marriage lawfully, and does not indulge in secret corruption, does well. And now enough has been said on these subjects.

Let anyone who will, take in his hand the Epistle to the Corinthians, and, examining all its passages one by one, then consider what we have said, comparing them together, as to whether there is not a perfect harmony and agreement between them. These things, according to my power, O Arete, I offer to thee as my contribution on the subject of chastity.

Euboulios. Through many things, O Gregorion, she has scarcely come to the subject, having measured and crossed a mighty sea of words.

Gregorion. So it seems; but come, I must mention the rest of what was said in order, going through it and repeating it, while I seem to have the sound of it dwelling in my ears, before it flies away and escapes; for the remembrance of things lately heard is easily effaced from the aged.

Euboulios. Say on, then; for we have come to have the pleasure of hearing these discourses.

Gregorion. And then after, as you observed, Thaleia had descended from her smooth and unbroken course to the earth, Theopatra, she said, followed her in order, and spoke as follows.

Discourse IV.—Theopatra.

Chapter I.—The Necessity of Praising Virtue, for Those Who Have the Power.

If the art of speaking, O virgins, always went by the same ways, and passed along the same path, there would be no way to avoid wearying you for one who persisted in the arguments which had already been urged. But since there are of arguments myriads of currents and ways, God inspiring us "at sundry times and in divers manners," who can have the choice of holding back or of being afraid? For he would not be free from blame to whom the gift has been given, if he failed to adorn that which is honorable with words of praise. Come then, we also, according to our gifts, will sing the brightest and most glorious star of Christ, which is chastity. For this way of the Spirit is very wide and large. Beginning, therefore, at the point from which we may say those things which are suitable and fitting to the subject before us, let us from thence consider it.

Chapter II.—The Protection of Chastity and Virginity Divinely Given to Men, that They May Emerge from the Mire of Vices.

Now I at least seem to perceive that nothing has been such a means of restoring men to paradise, and of the change to incorruption, and of reconciliation to God, and such a means of salvation to men, by guiding us to life, as chastity. And I will now endeavor to show why I think so concerning these things, that having heard distinctly the power of the grace already spoken of, you may know of how great blessings it has become the giver to us. Anciently, then, after the fall of man, when he was cast out by reason of his transgression, the stream of corruption poured forth abundantly, and running along in violent currents, not only fiercely swept along whatever touched it from without, but also rushing within it, overwhelmed the souls of men. And they, continuously exposed to this, were carried along dumb and stupid, neglecting to pilot their vessels, from having nothing firm to lay hold of. For the senses of the soul, as those have said who are learned in these things, when, being overcome by the excitements to passion which fall upon them from without, they receive the sudden bursts of the waves of folly which rush into them, being darkened turn aside from the divine course its whole vessel, which is by nature easily guided. Wherefore God, pitying us who were in such a condition, and were able neither to stand nor to rise, sent down from heaven the best and most glorious help, virginity, that by it we might tie our bodies fast, like ships, and have a calm, coming to an anchorage without damage, as also the Holy Spirit witnesses. For this is said in the hundred and thirty-sixth psalm, where the souls send joyfully up to God a hymn of thanksgiving, as many as have been taken hold of and raised up to walk with Christ in heaven, that they might not be overwhelmed by the streams of the world and the flesh. Whence, also, they say that Pharaoh was a type of the devil in Egypt, since he mercilessly commanded the males to be cast into the river, but the females to be preserved alive. For the devil, ruling from Adam to Moses over this great Egypt, the world, took care to have the male and rational offspring of the soul carried away and destroyed by the streams of passions, but he longs for the carnal and irrational offspring to increase and multiply.

Chapter III.—That Passage of David Explained; What the Harps Hung Upon the Willows Signify; The Willow a Symbol of Chastity; The Willows Watered by Streams.

But not to pass away from our subject, come, let us take in our hands and examine this psalm, which the pure and stainless souls sing to God, saying: "By the rivers of Babylon there we sat down; yea, we wept, when we remembered Zion. We hanged our harps upon the willows in the midst thereof," clearly giving the name of harps to their bodies which they hung upon the branches of chastity, fastening them to the wood that they might not be snatched away and dragged along again by the stream of incontinence. For Babylon, which is interpreted "disturbance" or "confusion," signifies this life around which the water flows, while we sit in the midst of which the water flows round us, as long as we are in the world, the rivers of evil always beating upon us. Wherefore, also, we are always fearful, and we groan and cry with weeping to God, that our harps may not be snatched off by the waves of pleasure, and slip down from the tree of chastity. For everywhere the divine writings take the willow as the type of chastity, because, when its flower is steeped in water, if it be drunk, it extinguishes whatever kindles sensual desires and passions within us, until it entirely renders barren, and makes every inclination to the begetting of children without effect, as also Homer indicated, for this reason calling the willows destructive of fruit. And in Isaiah the righteous are said to "spring up as willows by the water courses." Surely, then, the shoot of virginity is raised to a great and glorious height, when the righteous, and he to whom it is given to preserve it and to cultivate it, bedewing it with wisdom, is watered by the gentlest streams of Christ. For as it is the nature of this tree to bud and grow through water, so it is the nature of virginity to blossom and grow to maturity when enriched by words, so that one can hang his body2620 upon it.

Chapter IV.—The Author Goes on with the Interpretation of the Same Passage.

If, then, the rivers of Babylon are the streams of voluptuousness, as wise men say, which confuse and disturb the soul, then the willows must be chastity, to which we may suspend and draw up the organs of lust which overbalance and weigh down the mind, so that they may not be borne down by the torrents of incontinence, and be drawn like worms to impurity and corruption. For God has bestowed upon us virginity as a most useful and a serviceable help towards incorruption, sending it as an ally to those who are contending for and longing after Zion, as the psalm shows, which is resplendent charity and the commandment respecting it, for Zion is interpreted "The commandment of the watchtower." Now, let us here enumerate the points which follow. For why do the souls declare that they were asked by those who led them captive to sing the Lord's song in a strange land? Surely because the Gospel teaches a holy and secret song, which sinners and adulterers sing to the Evil One. For they insult the commandments, accomplishing the will of the spirits of evil, and cast holy things to dogs, and pearls before swine, in the same manner as those of whom the prophet says with indignation, "They read the law without;" for the Jews were not to read the law going forth out of the gates of Jerusalem or out of their houses; and for this reason the prophet blames them strongly, and cries that they were liable to condemnation, because, while they were transgressing the commandments, and acting impiously towards God, they were pretentiously reading the law, as if, forsooth, they were piously observing its precepts; but they did not receive it in their souls, holding it firmly with faith, but rejected it, denying it by their works. And hence they sing the Lord's song in a strange land, explaining the law by distorting and degrading it, expecting a sensual kingdom, and setting their hopes on this alien world, which the Word says will pass away, where those who carry them captive entice them with pleasures, lying in wait to deceive them.

Chapter V.—The Gifts of Virgins, Adorned with Which They are Presented to One Husband, Christ.

Now, those who sing the Gospel to senseless people seem to sing the Lord's song in a strange land, of which Christ is not the husbandman; but those who have put on and shone in the most pure and bright, and unmingled and pious and becoming, ornament of virginity, and are found barren and unproductive of unsettled and grievous passions, do not sing the song in a strange land; because they are not borne thither by their hopes, nor do they stick fast in the lusts of their mortal bodies, nor do they take a low view of the meaning of the commandments, but well and nobly, with a lofty disposition, they have regard to the promises which are above, thirsting for heaven as a congenial abode, whence God, approving their dispositions, promises with an oath to give them choice honors, appointing and establishing them "above His chief joy;" for He says thus: "If I forget thee, O Jerusalem, let my right hand forget her cunning. If I do not remember thee, let my tongue cleave to the roof of my mouth; if I prefer not Jerusalem above my chief joy;" meaning by Jerusalem, as I said, these very undefiled and incorrupt souls, which, having with self-denial drawn in the pure draught of virginity with unpolluted lips, are "espoused to one husband," to be presented "as a chaste virgin to Christ" in heaven, "having gotten the victory, striving for undefiled rewards." Hence also the prophet Isaiah proclaims, saying, "Arise, shine, for thy light is come, and the glory of the Lord is risen upon thee." Now these promises, it is evident to everyone, will be fulfilled after the resurrection. For the Holy Spirit does not speak of that well-known town in Judea; but truly of that heavenly city, the blessed Jerusalem, which He declares to be the assembly of the souls which God plainly promises to place first, "above His chief joy," in the new dispensation, settling those who are clothed in the most white robe of virginity in the pure dwelling of unapproachable light; because they had it not in mind to put off their wedding garment—that is, to relax their minds by wandering thoughts.

Chapter VI.—Virginity to Be Cultivated and Commended in Every Place and Time.

Further, the expression in Jeremiah, "That a maid should not forget her ornaments, nor a bride her attire," shows that she should not give up or loosen the band of chastity through wiles and distractions. For by the heart are properly denoted our heart and mind. Now the breast band, the girdle which gathers together and keeps firm the purpose of the soul to chastity, is love to God, which our Captain and Shepherd, Jesus, who is also our Ruler and Bridegroom, O illustrious virgins, commands both you and me to hold fast unbroken and sealed up even to the end; for one will not easily find anything else a greater help to men than this possession, pleasing and grateful to God. Therefore, I say, that we should all exercise and honor chastity, and always cultivate and commend it.

Let these first-fruits of my discourse suffice for thee, O Arete, in proof of my education and my zeal. "And I receive the gift," she said that Arete replied, "and bid Thallousa speak after thee; for I must have a discourse from each one of you." And she said that Thallousa, pausing a little, as though considering somewhat with herself, thus spoke.

Discourse V.—Thallousa.

Chapter I.—The Offering of Chastity a Great Gift.

I pray you, Arete, that you will give your assistance now too, that I may seem to speak something worthy in the first place of yourself, and then of those who are present. For I am persuaded, having thoroughly learnt it from the sacred writings, that the greatest and most glorious offering and gift, to which there is nothing comparable, which men can offer to God, is the life of virginity. For although many accomplished many admirable things, according to their vows, in the law, they alone were said to fulfil a great vow who were willing to offer themselves of their free-will. For the passage runs thus: "And the Lord spoke unto Moses, saying, Speak unto the children of Israel, and say unto them, when either man or woman shall separate themselves…unto the Lord." One vows to offer gold and silver vessels for the sanctuary when he comes, another to offer the tithe of his fruits, another of his property, another the best of his flocks, another consecrates his being; and no one is able to vow a great vow to the Lord, but he who has offered himself entirely to God.

Chapter II.—Abraham's Sacrifice of a Heifer Three Years Old, of a Goat, and of a Ram Also Three Years Old: Its Meaning; Every Age to Be Consecrated to God; The Threefold Watch and Our Age.

I must endeavor, O virgins, by a true exposition, to explain to you the mind of the Scripture according to its meaning. Now, he who watches over and restrains himself in part, and in part is distracted and wandering, is not wholly given up to God. Hence it is necessary that the perfect man offer up all, both the things of the soul and those of the flesh, so that he may be complete and not lacking. Therefore also God commands Abraham, "Take Me an heifer of three years old, and a she goat of three years old, and a ram of three years old, and a turtle dove, and a young pigeon;" which is admirably said; for remark, that concerning those things, He also gives this command, Bring them Me and keep them free from the yoke, even thy soul uninjured, like a heifer, and your flesh, and your reason; the last like a goat, since he traverses lofty and precipitous places, and the other like a ram, that he may in nowise skip away, and fall and slip off from the right way. For thus shalt thou be perfect and blameless, O Abraham, when thou hast offered to Me thy soul, and thy sense, and thy mind, which He mentioned under the symbol of the heifer, the goat, and the ram of three years old, as though they represented the pure knowledge of the Trinity.

And perhaps He also symbolizes the beginning, the middle, and the end of our life and of our age, wishing as far as possible that men should spend their boyhood, their manhood, and their more advanced life purely, and offer them up to Him. Just as our Lord Jesus Christ commands in the Gospels, thus directing: "Let not your lights be extinguished, and let not your loins be loosed. Therefore also be ye like men who wait for their lord, when he will return from the wedding; that, when he comes and knocks, they may open unto him immediately. Blessed are ye, when he shall make you sit down, and shall come and serve you. And if he come in the second, or in the third watch, ye are blessed." For consider, O virgins, when He mentions three watches of the night, and His three comings, He shadows forth in symbol our three periods of life, that of the boy, of the full-grown man, and of the old man; so that if He should come and remove us from the world while spending our first period, that is, while we are boys, He may receive us ready and pure, having nothing amiss; and the second and the third in like manner. For the evening watch is the time of the budding and youth of man, when the reason begins to be disturbed and to be clouded by the changes of life, his flesh gaining strength and urging him to lust. The second is the time when, afterwards advancing to a full-grown man, he begins to acquire stability, and to make a stand against the turbulence of passion and self-conceit. And the third, when most of the imaginations and desires fade away, the flesh now withering and declining to old age.

Chapter III.—Far Best to Cultivate Virtue from Boyhood.

Therefore, it is becoming that we should kindle the unquenchable light of faith in the heart, and gird our loins with purity, and watch and ever wait for the Lord so that, if He should will to come and take any of us away in the first period of life, or in the second, or in the third, and should find us most ready, and working what He appointed, He may make us to lie down in the bosom of Abraham, of Isaac, and of Jacob. Now Jeremiah says, "It is good for a man that he bear the yoke in his youth;" and "that his soul should not depart from the Lord." It is good, indeed, from boyhood, to submit the neck to the divine Hand, and not to shake off, even to old age, the Rider who guides with pure mind, when the Evil One is ever dragging down the mind to that which is worse. For who is there that does not receive through the eyes, through the ears, through the taste and smell and touch, pleasures and delights, so as to become impatient of the control of continence as a driver, who checks and vehemently restrains the horse from evil? Another who turns his thoughts to other things will think differently; but we say that he offers himself perfectly to God who strives to keep the flesh undefiled from childhood, practicing virginity; for it speedily brings great and much-desired gifts of hopes to those who strive for it, drying up the corrupting lusts and passions of the soul. But come, let us explain how we give ourselves up to the Lord.

Chapter IV.—Perfect Consecration and Devotion to God: What It is.

That which is laid down in the Book of Numbers, "greatly to vow a vow," serves to show, as, with a little more explanation, I proceed to prove, that chastity is the great vow above all vows. For then am I plainly consecrated altogether to the Lord, when I not only strive to keep the flesh untouched by intercourse, but also unspotted by other kinds of unseemliness. For "the unmarried woman," it is said, "cares for the things of the

Lord, how she may please the Lord.;" not merely that she may bear away the glory in part of not being maimed in her virtue, but in both parts, according to the apostle, that she may be sanctified in body and spirit, offering up her members to the Lord. For let us say what it is to offer up oneself perfectly to the Lord. If, for instance, I open my mouth on some subjects, and close it upon others; thus, if I open it for the explanation of the Scriptures, for the praise of God, according to my power, in a true faith and with all due honor, and if I close it, putting a door and a watch upon it against foolish discourse, my mouth is kept pure, and is offered up to God. "My tongue is a pen," an organ of wisdom; for the Word of the Spirit writes by it in clearest letters, from the depth and power of the Scriptures, even the Lord, the swift Writer of the ages, that He quickly and swiftly registers and fulfils the counsel of the Father, hearing the words, "quickly spoil, swiftly plunder." To such a Scribe the words may be applied, "My tongue is a pen;" for a beautiful pen is sanctified and offered to Him, writing things more lovely than the poets and orators who confirm the doctrines of men. If, too, I accustom my eyes not to lust after the charms of the body, nor to take delight in unseemly sights, but to look up to the things which are above, then my eyes are kept pure, and are offered to the Lord. If I shut my ears against detraction and slanders, and open them to the word of God, having intercourse with wise men, then have I offered up my ears to the Lord. If I keep my hands from dishonorable dealing, from acts of covetousness and of licentiousness, then are my hands kept pure to God. If I withhold my steps from going in perverse ways, then have I offered up my feet, not going to the places of public resort and banquets, where wicked men are found, but into the right way, fulfilling something of the commands. What, then, remains to me, if I also keep the heart pure, offering up all its thoughts to God; if I think no evil, if anger and wrath gain no rule over me, if I meditate in the law of the Lord day and night? And this is to preserve a great chastity, and to vow a great vow.

Chapter V.—The Vow of Chastity, and Its Rites in the Law; Vines, Christ, and the Devil.

I will now endeavor to explain to you, O virgins, the rest of that which is prescribed; for this is attached to your duties, consisting of laws concerning virginity, which are useful as teaching how we should abstain, and how advance to virginity. For it is written thus: "And the Lord spoke unto Moses, saying, Speak unto the children of Israel, and say unto them, When either man or woman shall separate themselves to vow a vow of a Nazarite, to separate themselves unto the Lord; he shall separate himself from wine and strong drink, and shall drink no vinegar of wine, or vinegar of strong drink, neither shall he drink any liquor of grapes, nor eat moist grapes, or dried, all the days of his separation." And this means, that he who has devoted and offered himself to the Lord shall not take of the fruits of the plant of evil, because of its natural tendency to produce intoxication and distraction of mind. For we perceive from the Scriptures two kinds of vines which were separate from each other, and were unlike. For the one is productive of immortality and righteousness; but the other of madness and insanity. The sober and joy-producing vine, from whose instructions, as from branches, there joyfully hang down clusters of graces, distilling love, is our Lord Jesus, who says expressly to the apostles, "I am the true vine, ye are the branches; and my Father is the husbandman." But the wild and death-bearing vine is the devil, who drops down fury and poison and wrath, as Moses relates, writing concerning him, "For their vine is of the vine of Sodom, and of the fields of Gomorrah: their grapes are grapes of gall, their clusters are bitter: their wine is the poison of dragons, and the cruel venom of asps." The inhabitants of Sodom having gathered grapes from this, were goaded on to an unnatural and fruitless desire for males. Hence, also, in the time of Noah, men having given themselves up to drunkenness, sank down into unbelief, and, being overwhelmed by the deluge, were drowned. And Cain, too, having drawn from this, stained his fratricidal hands, and defiled the earth with the blood of his own family. Hence, too, the heathen, becoming intoxicated, sharpen their passions for murderous battles; for man is not so much excited, nor goes so far astray through wine, as from anger and wrath. A man does not become intoxicated and go astray through wine, in the same way as he does from sorrow, or from love, or from incontinence. And therefore it is ordered that a virgin shall not taste of this vine, so that she may be sober and watchful from the cares of life, and may kindle the shining torch of the light of righteousness for the Word. "Take heed to yourselves," says the Lord, "lest at any time your hearts be overcharged with surfeiting, and drunkenness, and cares of this life, and so that day come upon you unawares, as a snare."

Chapter VI.—Sikera, a Manufactured and Spurious Wine, Yet Intoxicating; Things Which are Akin to Sins are to Be Avoided by a Virgin; The Altar of Incense (a Symbol Of) Virgins.

Moreover, it is not only forbidden to virgins in any way to touch those things which are made from that vine, but even such things as resemble them and are akin to them. For Sikera, which is manufactured, is called a spurious kind of wine, whether made of palms or of other fruit-trees. For in the same way that draughts of wine overthrow man's reason, so do these exceedingly; and to speak the plain truth, the wise are accustomed to call by the name of Sikera all that produces drunkenness and distraction of mind, besides wine. In order, therefore, that the virgin may not, when guarding against those sins which are in their own nature evil, be defiled by those which are like them and akin to them, conquering the one and being conquered by the other, that is, decorating herself with textures of different cloths, or with stones and gold, and other decorations of the body, things which intoxicate the soul; on this account it is ordered that she do not give herself up to womanish weaknesses and laughter, exciting herself to wiles and foolish talking, which whirl the mind around and confuse it; as it is indicated in another place, "Ye shall not eat the hyena and animals like it; nor the weasel and creatures of that kind." For this is the straight and direct way to heaven, not merely not to avoid any stumbling-block which would trip up and destroy men who are agitated by a desire for luxuries and pleasures, but also from such things as resemble them.

Moreover, it has been handed down that the unbloody altar of God signifies the assembly of the chaste; thus virginity appears to be something great and glorious. Therefore it ought to be preserved undefiled and altogether pure, having no participation in the impurities of the flesh; but it should be set up before the presence of the testimony, gilded with wisdom, for the Holy of holies, sending forth a sweet savor of love to the Lord; for He says, "Thou shalt make an altar to burn incense upon: of shittim-wood shalt thou make it. And thou shalt make the staves of shittim-wood, and overlay them with gold. And thou shalt put it before the veil that is by the ark of the testimony, before the mercy-seat that is over the testimony, where I will meet with thee. And Aaron shall burn thereon sweet incense every morning: when he dresses the lamps, he shall burn incense upon it. And when Aaron lighted the lamps at even, he shall burn incense upon it; a perpetual incense before the Lord throughout your generations. Ye shall offer no strange incense thereon, nor burnt-sacrifices nor meat-offering; neither shall ye pour drink-offering thereon."

Chapter VII.—The Church Intermediate Between the Shadows of the Law and the Realities of Heaven.

If the law, according to the apostle, is spiritual, containing the images "of future good things," come then, let us strip off the veil of the letter which is spread over it, and consider its naked and true meaning. The Hebrews were commanded to ornament the Tabernacle as a type of the Church, that they might be able, by means of sensible things, to announce beforehand the image of divine things. For the pattern which was shown to Moses in the mount, to which he was to have regard in fashioning the Tabernacle, was a kind of accurate representation of the heavenly dwelling, which we now perceive more clearly than through types, yet more darkly than if we saw the reality. For not yet, in our present condition, has the truth come unmingled to men, who are here unable to bear the sight of pure immortality, just as we cannot bear to look upon the rays of the sun. And the Jews declared that the shadow of the image (of the heavenly things which was afforded to them), was the third from the reality; but we clearly behold the image of the heavenly order; for the truth will be accurately made manifest after the resurrection, when we shall see the heavenly tabernacle (the city in heaven "whose builder and maker is God") "face to face," and not "darkly" and "in part."

Chapter VIII.—The Double Altar, Widows and Virgins; Gold the Symbol of Virginity.

Now the Jews prophesied our state, but we foretell the heavenly; since the Tabernacle was a symbol of the Church, and the Church of heaven. Therefore, these things being so, and the Tabernacle being taken for a type of the Church, as I said, it is fitting that the altars should signify some of the things in the Church. And we have already compared the brazen altar to the company and circuit of widows; for they are a living altar of God, to which they bring calves and tithes, and free-will offerings, as a sacrifice to the Lord; but the golden altar within the Holy of holies, before the presence of the testimony, on which it is forbidden to offer sacrifice and libation, has reference to those in a state of virginity, as those who have their bodies preserved pure, like unalloyed gold, from carnal intercourse. Now gold is commended for two reasons: the first, that it does not rust, and the second, that in its color it seems in a measure to resemble the rays of the sun; and thus it is suitably a symbol of virginity, which does not admit any stain or spot, but ever shines forth with the light of the Word. Therefore, also, it stands nearer *to God* within the Holy of holies, and before the veil, with undefiled hands, like incense, offering up prayers to the Lord, acceptable as a sweet savor; as also John indicated, saying that the incense in the vials of the four-and-twenty elders were the prayers of the saints. This, then, I offer to thee, O Arete, on the spur of the moment, according to my ability, on the subject of chastity.

And when Thallousa had said this, Theopatra said that Arete touched Agathe with her scepter, and that she, perceiving it, immediately arose and answered.

Discourse VI.—Agathe.
Chapter I.—The Excellence of the Abiding Glory of Virginity; The Soul Made in the Image of the Image of God, that is of His Son; The Devil a Suitor for the Soul.

With great confidence of being able to persuade, and to carry on this admirable discourse, O Arete, if thou go with me, will I also endeavor, according to my ability, to contribute something to the discussion of the subject before us; something commensurate to my own power, and not to be compared with that which has already been spoken. For I should be unable to put forth in philosophizing anything that could compete with those things which have already been so variously and brilliantly worked out. For I shall seem to bear away the reproach of silliness, if I make an effort to match myself with my superiors in wisdom. If, however, you will bear even with those who speak as they can, I will endeavor to speak, not lacking at least in good will. And here let me begin.

We have all come into this world, O virgins, endowed with singular beauty, which has a relationship and affinity to *divine* wisdom. For the souls of men do then most accurately resemble Him who begat and formed them, when, reflecting the unsullied representation of His likeness, and the features of that countenance, to which God looking formed them to have an immortal and indestructible shape, they remain such. For the unbegotten and incorporeal beauty, which neither begins nor is corruptible, but is unchangeable, and grows not old and has need of nothing, He resting in Himself, and in the very light which is in unspeakable and inapproachable places, embracing all things in the circumference of His power, creating and arranging, made the soul after the image of His image. Therefore, also, it is reasonable and immortal. For being made after the image of the Only-begotten, as I said, it has an unsurpassable beauty, and therefore evil spirits love it, and plot and strive to defile its godlike and lovely image, as the prophet Jeremiah shows, reproaching Jerusalem, "Thou has a whore's forehead, thou refuses to be ashamed;" speaking of her who prostituted herself to the powers which came against her to pollute her. For her lovers are the devil and his angels, who plan to defile and pollute our reasonable and clear-sighted beauty of mind by intercourse with themselves, and desire to cohabit with every soul which is betrothed to the Lord.

Chapter II.—The Parable of the Ten Virgins.

If, then, anyone will keep this beauty inviolate and unharmed, and such as He who constructed it formed and fashioned it, imitating the eternal and intelligible nature of which man is the representation and likeness, and will become like a glorious and holy image, he will be transferred thence to heaven, the city of the blessed, and will dwell there as in a sanctuary. Now our beauty is then best preserved undefiled and perfect when, protected by virginity, it is not darkened by the heat of corruption from without; but, remaining in itself, it is adorned with righteousness, being brought as a bride to the Son of God; as He also Himself suggests, exhorting that the light of chastity should be kindled in their flesh, as in lamps; since the number of the ten virgins s signifies the souls that have believed in Jesus Christ, symbolizing by the ten the only right way to heaven. Now five of them were prudent and wise; and five were foolish and unwise, for they had not the forethought to fill their vessels with oil, remaining destitute of righteousness. Now by these He signifies those who strive to come to the boundaries of virginity, and who strain every nerve to fulfil this love, acting virtuously and temperately, and who profess and boast that this is their aim; but who, making light of it, and being subdued by the changes of the world, come rather to be sketches of the shadowy image of virtue, than workers who represent the living truth itself.

Chapter III.—The Same Endeavour and Effort After Virginity, with a Different Result.

Now when it is said that "the kingdom of heaven is likened unto ten virgins, which took their lamps and went forth to meet the bridegroom," this means that the same way towards the goal had been entered upon, as is shown by the mark X. By profession they had equally proposed the same end, and therefore they are called ten, since, as I have said, they chose the same profession; but they did not, for all that, go forth in the same way to meet the bridegroom. For some provided abundant future nourishment for their lamps which were fed with oil, but others were careless, thinking only of the present. And, therefore, they are divided into two equal numbers of five, inasmuch as the one class preserved the five senses, which most people consider the gates of wisdom, pure and undefiled by sins; but the others, on the contrary, corrupted them by multitudes of sins, defiling themselves with evil. For having restrained them, and kept them free from righteousness, they bore a more abundant crop of transgressions, in consequence of which it came to pass that they were forbidden, and shut out from the divine courts. For whether, on the one hand, we do right, or, on the other, do wrong through these senses, our habits of good and evil are confirmed. And as Thallousa said that there is a chastity of the eyes, and of the ears, and of the tongue, and so on of the other senses; so here she who keeps inviolate the faith of the five pathways of virtue—sight, taste, smell, touch, and hearing—is called by the name of the five virgins, because she has kept the five forms of the sense pure to Christ, as a lamp, causing the light of holiness to shine forth clearly from each of them. For the flesh is truly, as it were, our five-lighted lamp, which the soul will bear like a torch, when it stands before Christ the Bridegroom, on the day of the resurrection, showing her faith springing out clear and bright through all the senses, as He Himself taught, saying, "I am come to send fire on the earth; and what will I if it be already kindled?" meaning by the earth our bodies, in which He wished the swift-moving and fiery operation of His doctrine to be kindled. Now the oil represents wisdom and righteousness; for while the soul rains down unsparingly, and pours forth these things upon the body, the light of virtue is kindled unquenchably, making its good actions to shine before men, so that our Father which is in heaven may be glorified.

Chapter IV.—What the Oil in the Lamps Means.

Now they offered, in Leviticus, oil of this kind, "pure oil olive, beaten for the light, to cause the lamps to burn continually, without the veil...before the Lord." But they were commanded to have a feeble light from the evening to the morning. For their light seemed to resemble the prophetic word, which gives encouragement to temperance, being nourished by the acts and the faith of the people. But the temple (in which the light was kept burning) refers to "the lot of their inheritance," inasmuch as a light can shine in only one house. Therefore it was necessary that it should be lighted before day. For he says, *they shall burn it* until the morning," that is, until the coming of Christ. But the Sun of chastity and of righteousness having arisen, there is no need of *other* light.

So long, then, as this people treasured up nourishment for the light, supplying oil by their works, the light of continence was not extinguished among them, but was ever shining and giving light in the "lot of their inheritance." But when the oil failed, by their turning away from the faith to incontinence, the light was entirely extinguished, so that the virgins have again to kindle their lamps by light transmitted from one to another, bringing the light of incorruption to the world from above. Let us then supply now the oil of good works abundantly, and of prudence, being purged from all corruption which would weigh us down; lest, while the Bridegroom tarries, our lamps may also in like manner be extinguished. For the delay is the interval which precedes the appearing of Christ. Now the slumbering and sleeping of the virgins signifies the departure from life; and the midnight is the kingdom of Antichrist, during which the destroying angel passes over the houses. But the cry which was made when it was said, "Behold the bridegroom cometh, go ye out to meet him," is the voice which shall be heard from heaven, and the trumpet, when the saints, all their bodies being raised, shall be caught up, and shall go on the clouds to meet the Lord.

For it is to be observed that the word *of God* says, that after the cry all the virgins arose, that is, that the dead shall be raised after the voice which comes from heaven, as also Paul intimates, that "the Lord Himself shall descend from heaven with a shout, with the voice of the archangel, and with the trump of God: and the dead in Christ shall rise first;" that is the tabernacles, for they died, being put off by their souls. "Then we which are alive shall be caught up together with them," meaning our souls. For we truly who are alive are the souls which, with the bodies, having put them on again, shall go to meet Him in the clouds, bearing our lamps trimmed, not with anything alien and worldly, but like stars radiating the light of prudence and continence, full of ethereal splendor.

Chapter V.—The Reward of Virginity.

These, O fair virgins, are the orgies of our mysteries; these the mystic rites of those who are initiated in virginity; these the "undefiled rewards" of the conflict of virginity. I am betrothed to the Word, and receive as a reward the eternal crown of immortality and riches from the Father; and I triumph in eternity, crowned with the bright and unfading flowers of wisdom. I am one in the choir with Christ dispensing His rewards in heaven, around the unbeginning and never-ending King. I have become the torch-bearer of the unapproachable lights, and

I join with their company in the new song of the archangels, showing forth the new grace of the Church; for the Word says that the company of virgins always follow the Lord, and have fellowship with Him wherever He is. And this is what John signifies in the commemoration of the hundred and forty-four thousand.

Go then, ye virgin band of the new ages. Go, fill your vessels with righteousness, for the hour is coming when ye must rise and meet the bridegroom. Go, lightly leaving on one side the fascinations and the pleasures of life, which confuse and bewitch the soul; and thus shall ye attain the promises, "This I swear by Him who has shown me the way of life." This crown, woven by the prophets, I have taken from the prophetic meadows, and offer to thee, O Arete. Agathe having thus admirably brought her discourse to an end, she said, and having been applauded for what she had uttered, Arete again commanded Procilla to speak. And she, rising and passing before the entrance, spoke thus.

Discourse VII.—Procilla.
Chapter I.—What the True and Seemly Manner of Praising; The Father Greater Than the Son, Not in Substance, But in Order; Virginity the Lily; Faithful Souls and Virgins, the One Bride of the One Christ.

It is not lawful for me to delay, O Arete, after such discourses, seeing that I confide undoubtingly in the manifold wisdom of God, which gives richly and widely to whomsoever it wills. For sailors who have experience of the sea declare that the same wind blows on all who sail; and that different persons, managing their course differently, strive to reach different ports. Some have a fair wind; to others it blows across their course; and yet both easily accomplish their voyage. Now, in the same way, the "understanding Spirit, holy, one only," gently breathing down from the treasures of the Father above, giving us all the clear fair wind of knowledge, will suffice to guide the course of our words without offence. And now it is time for me to speak. This, O virgins, is the one true and seemly mode of praising, when he who praises brings forward a witness better than all those who are praised. For thence one may learn with certainty that the commendation is given not from favor, nor of necessity, nor from repute, but in accordance with truth and an unflattering judgment. And so the prophets and apostles, who spoke more fully concerning the Son of God, and assigned to Him a divinity above other men, did not refer their praises of Him to the teaching of angels, but to Him upon whom all authority and power depend. For it was fitting that He who was greater than all things after the Father, should have the Father, who alone is greater than Himself, as His witness. And so I will not bring forward the praises of virginity from mere human report, but from Him who cares for us, and who has taken up the whole matter, showing that He is the husbandman of this grace, and a lover of its beauty, and a fitting witness. And this is quite clear, in the Song of Songs, to anyone who is willing to see it, where Christ Himself, praising those who are firmly established in virginity, says, "As the lily among thorns, so is my love among the daughters;" comparing the grace of chastity to the lily, on account of its purity and fragrance, and sweetness and joyousness. For chastity is like a spring flower, always softly exhaling immortality from its white petals. Therefore He is not ashamed to confess that He loves the beauty of its prime, in the following words: "Thou hast ravished my heart, my sister, my spouse; thou hast ravished my heart with one of thine eyes, with one chain of thy neck. How fair is thy love, my sister, my spouse! How much better is thy love than wine! And the smell of thine ointments than all spices! Thy lips, O my spouse, drop as the honeycomb; honey and milk are under thy tongue; and the smell of thy garments is like the smell of Lebanon. A garden enclosed is my sister, my spouse; a spring shut up, a fountain sealed."

These praises does Christ proclaim to those who have come to the boundaries of virginity, describing them all under the one name of His spouse; for the spouse must be betrothed to the Bridegroom, and called by His name. And, moreover, she must be undefiled and unpolluted, as a garden sealed, in which all the odors of the fragrance of heaven are grown, that Christ alone may come and gather them, blooming with incorporeal seeds. For the Word loves none of the things of the flesh, because He is not of such a nature as to be contented with any of the things which are corruptible, as hands, or face, or feet; but He looks upon and delights in the beauty which is immaterial and spiritual, not touching the beauty of the body.

Chapter II.—The Interpretation of that Passage of the Canticles.

Consider now, O virgins, that, in saying to the bride, "Thou hast ravished my heart, my sister, my spouse," He shows the clear eye of the understanding, when the inner man has cleansed it and looks more clearly upon the truth. For it is clear to everyone that there is a twofold power of sight, the one of the soul, and the other of the body. But the Word does not profess a love for that of the body, but only that of the understanding, saying,

"Thou hast ravished my heart with one of thine eyes, with one chain of thy neck;" which means, By the most lovely sight of thy mind, thou hast urged my heart to love, radiating forth from within the glorious beauty of chastity. Now the chains of the neck are necklaces which are composed of various precious stones; and the souls which take care of the body, place around the outward neck of the flesh this visible ornament to deceive those who behold; but those who live chastely, on the other hand, adorn themselves within with ornaments truly composed of various precious stones, namely, of freedom, of magnanimity, of wisdom, and of love, caring little for those temporal decorations which, like leaves blossoming for an hour, dry up with the changes of the body. For there is seen in man a twofold beauty, of which the Lord accepts that which is within and is immortal, saying, "Thou hast ravished my heart with one chain of thy neck;" meaning to show that He had been drawn to love by the splendor of the inner man shining forth in its glory, even as the Psalmist also testifies, saying, "The King's daughter is all glorious within."

Chapter III.—Virgins Being Martyrs First Among the Companions of Christ.

Let no one suppose that all the remaining company of those who have believed are condemned, thinking that we who are virgins alone shall be led on to attain the promises, not understanding that there shall be tribes and families and orders, according to the analogy of the faith of each. And this Paul, too, sets forth, saying, "There is one glory of the sun, and another glory of the moon, and another glory of the stars: for one star differed from another star in glory. So also is the resurrection of the dead." And the Lord does not profess to give the same honors to all; but to some He promises that they shall be numbered in the kingdom of heaven, to others the inheritance of the earth, and to others to see the Father. And here, also, He announces that the order and holy choir of the virgins shall first enter in company with Him into the rest of the new dispensation, as into a bridal chamber. For they were martyrs, not as bearing the pains of the body for a little moment of time, but as enduring them through all their life, not shrinking from truly wrestling in an Olympian contest for the prize of chastity; but resisting the fierce torments of pleasures and fears and griefs, and the other evils of the iniquity of men, they first of all carry off the prize, taking their place in the higher rank of those who receive the promise. Undoubtedly these are the souls whom the Word calls alone His chosen spouse and His sister, but the rest concubines and virgins and daughters, speaking thus: "There are threescore queens and fourscore concubines, and virgins without number. My dove, my undefiled, is but one; she is the only one of her mother, she is the choice one of her that bare her: the daughters saw her and blessed her: yea, the queens and the concubines, and they praised her." For there being plainly many daughters of the Church, one alone is the chosen and most precious in her eyes above all, namely, the order of virgins.

Chapter IV.—The Passage Explained; The Queens, the Holy Souls Before the Deluge; The Concubines, the Souls of the Prophets; The Divine Seed for Spiritual Offspring in the Books of the Prophets; The Nuptials of the Word in the Prophets as Though Clandestine.

Now if anyone should have a doubt about these things, inasmuch as the points are nowhere fully wrought out, and should still wish more fully to perceive their spiritual significance, namely, what the queens and the concubines and the virgins are, we will say that these may have been spoken concerning those who have been conspicuous for their righteousness from the beginning throughout the progress of time; as of those before the flood, and those after the flood, and so on of those after Christ. The Church, then, is the spouse. The queens are those royal souls before the deluge, who became well-pleasing to God, that is, those about Abel and Seth and Enoch. The concubines those after the flood, namely, those of the prophets, in whom, before the Church was betrothed to the Lord, being united to them after the manner of concubines, He sowed true words in an incorrupt and pure philosophy, so that, conceiving faith, they might bring forth to Him the Spirit of salvation. For such fruits do the souls bring forth with whom Christ has had intercourse, fruits which bear an ever-memorable renown. For if you will look at the books of Moses, or David, or Solomon, or Isaiah, or of the prophets who follow, O virgins, you will see what offspring they have left, for the saving of life, from their intercourse with the Son of God. Hence the Word has with deep perception called the souls of the prophets concubines, because He did not espouse them openly, as He did the Church, having killed for her the fatted calf.

Chapter V.—The Sixty Queens: Why Sixty, and Why Queens; The Excellence of the Saints of the First Age.

In addition to these matters, there is this also to be considered, so that nothing may escape us of things which are necessary, why He said that the queens were sixty, and the concubines eighty, and the virgins so numerous as not to be counted from their multitude, but the spouse one. And first let us speak of the sixty. I imagine that He named under the sixty queens, those who had pleased God from the first-made man in succession to Noah, for this reason, since these had no need of precepts and laws for their salvation, the creation of the world in six days being still recent. For they remembered that in six days God formed the creation, and those things which were made in paradise; and how man, receiving a command not to touch the tree of knowledge, ran aground, the author of evil having led him astray. Thence he gave the symbolical name of sixty queens to those souls who, from the creation of the world, in succession chose God as the object of their love, and were almost, so to speak, the offspring of the first age, and neighbors of the great six days' work, from their having been born, as I said, immediately after the six days. For these had great honor, being associated with the angels, and often seeing God manifested visibly, and not in a dream. For consider what confidence Seth had towards God, and Abel, and Enos, and Enoch, and Methuselah, and Noah, the first lovers of righteousness, and the first of the first-born children who are written in heaven, being thought worthy of the kingdom, as a kind of first-fruits of the plants for salvation, coming out as early fruit to God. And so much may suffice concerning these.

Chapter VI.—The Eighty Concubines, What; The Knowledge of the Incarnation Communicated to the Prophets.

It still remains to speak concerning the concubines. To those who lived after the deluge the knowledge of God was henceforth more remote, and they needed other instruction to ward off the evil, and to be their helper, since idolatry was already creeping in. Therefore God, that the race of man might not be wholly destroyed, through forgetfulness of the things which were good, commanded His own Son to reveal to the prophets His own future appearance in the world by the flesh, in which the joy and knowledge of the spiritual eighth day shall be proclaimed, which would bring the remission of sins and the resurrection, and that thereby the passions and corruptions of men would be circumcised. And, therefore, He called by the name of the eighty virgins the list of the prophets from Abraham, on account of the dignity of circumcision, which embraces the number eight, in accordance with which also the law is framed; because they first, before the Church was espoused to the Word, received the divine seed, and foretold the circumcision of the spiritual eighth day.

Chapter VII.—The Virgins, the Righteous Ancients; The Church, the One Only Spouse, More Excellent Than the Others.

Now he calls by the name of virgins, who belong to a countless assembly, those who, being inferior to the better ones, have practiced righteousness, and have striven against sin with youthful and noble energy. But of these, neither the queens, nor the concubines, nor the virgins, are compared to the Church. For she is reckoned the perfect and chosen one beyond all these, consisting and composed of all the apostles, the Bride who surpasses all in the beauty of youth and virginity. Therefore, also, she is blessed and praised by all, because she saw and heard freely what those desired to see, even for a little time, and saw not, and to hear, but heard not. For "blessed," said our Lord to His disciples, "are your eyes, for they see; and your ears, for they hear. For verily I say unto you, That many prophets have desired to see those things which ye see, and have not seen them; and to hear those things which ye hear, and have not heard them." For this reason, then, the prophets count them blessed, and admire them, because the Church was thought worthy to participate in those things which they did not attain to hear or see. For "there are threescore queens, and fourscore concubines, and virgins without number. My dove, my undefiled, is but one."

Chapter VIII.—The Human Nature of Christ His One Dove.

Can anyone now say otherwise than that the Bride is the undefiled flesh of the Lord, for the sake of which He left the Father and came down here, and was joined to it, and, being incarnate, dwelt in it? Therefore He called it figuratively a dove, because that creature is tame and domestic, and readily adapts itself to man's mode of life. For she alone, so to speak, was found spotless and undefiled, and excelling all in the glory and beauty of righteousness, so that none of those who had pleased God most perfectly could stand near to her in a comparison of virtue. And for this reason she was thought worthy to become a partaker of the kingdom of the Only-begotten, being betrothed and united to Him. And in the forty-fourth psalm, the queen who, chosen out of many, stands at the right hand of God, clothed in the golden ornament of virtue, whose beauty the King desired, is, as I said, the undefiled and blessed flesh, which the Word Himself carried into the heavens, and presented at the right hand of God, "wrought about with divers colors," that is, in the pursuits of immortality, which he calls symbolically golden fringes. For since this garment is variegated and woven of various virtues, as chastity, prudence, faith, love, patience, and other good things, which, covering, as they do, the unseemliness of the flesh, adorn man with a golden ornament.

Chapter IX.—The Virgins Immediately After the Queen and Spouse.

Moreover, we must further consider what the Spirit delivers to us in the rest of the psalm, after the enthronization of the manhood assumed by the Word at the right hand of the Father. "The virgins," He says, "that be her fellows shall bear her company, and shall be brought unto thee. With joy and gladness shall they be brought, and shall enter into the King's palace." Now, here the Spirit seems quite plainly to praise virginity, next, as we have explained, to the Bride of the Lord, who promises that the virgins shall approach second to the Almighty with joy and gladness, guarded and escorted by angels. For so lovely and desirable is in truth the glory of virginity, that, next to the Queen, whom the Lord exalts, and presents in sinless glory to the Father, the choir and order of virgins bear her company, assigned to a place second to that of the Bride. Let these efforts of mine to speak to thee, O Arete, concerning chastity, be engraven on a monument.

And Procilla having thus spoken, Thekla said, it is my turn after her to continue the contest; and I rejoice, since I too have the favoring wisdom of words, perceiving that I am, like a harp, inwardly attuned, and prepared to speak with elegance and propriety.

Arete. I most willingly hail thy readiness, O Thekla, in which I confide to give me fitting discourse, in accordance with thy powers; since thou wilt yield to none in universal philosophy and instruction, instructed by Paul in what is fitting to say of evangelical and divine doctrine.

Discourse VIII.—Thekla.
Chapter I.—Methodius' Derivation of the Word Virginity: Wholly Divine; Virtue, in Greek—ἀρετή, Whence So Called.

Well, then, let us first say, beginning from the origin of the name, for what cause this supreme and blessed pursuit was called παρθενία, what it aims at, what power it has, and afterwards, what fruits it gives forth. For almost all have been ignorant of this virtue as being superior to ten thousand other advantages of virtue which we cultivate for the purification and adornment of the soul. For virginity is divine by the change of one letter, as she alone makes him who has her, and is initiated by her incorruptible rites like unto God, than which it is impossible to find a greater good, removed, as it is, from pleasure and grief; and the wing of the soul sprinkled by it becomes stronger and lighter, accustomed daily to fly from human desires.

For since the children of the wise have said that our life is a festival, and that we have come to exhibit in the theatre the drama of truth, that is, righteousness, the devil and the demons plotting and striving against us, it is necessary for us to look upwards and to take our flight aloft, and to flee from the blandishments of their tongues, and from their forms tinged with the outward appearance of temperance, more than from the Sirens of Homer. For many, bewitched by the pleasures of error, take their flight downwards, and are weighed down when they come into this life, their nerves being relaxed and unstrung, by means of which the power of the wings of temperance is strengthened, lightening the downward tendency of the corruption of the body. Whence, O Arete, whether thou hast thy name, *signifying virtue*, because thou art worthy of being chosen for thyself, or because thou raises and lifts up to heaven, ever going in the purest minds, come, give me thy help in my discourse, which thou hast thyself appointed me to speak.

Chapter II.—The Lofty Mind and Constancy of the Sacred Virgins; The Introduction of Virgins into the Blessed Abodes Before Others.

Those who take a downward flight, and fall into pleasures, do not desist from grief and labors until, through their passionate desires, they fulfil the want of their intemperance, and, being degraded and shut out from the sanctuary, they are removed from the scene of truth, and, instead of procreating children with modesty and temperance, they rave in the wild pleasures of unlawful amours. But those who, on light wing, ascend into the supramundane life, and see from afar what other men do not see, the very pastures of immortality, bearing in abundance flowers of inconceivable beauty, are ever turning themselves again to the spectacles there; and, for this reason, those things are thought small which are here considered noble—such as wealth, and glory, and birth, and marriage; and they think no more of those things. But yet if any of them should choose to give up their bodies to wild beasts or to fire, and be punished, they are ready to have no care for pains, for the desire of them or the fear of them; so that they seem, while in the world, not to be in the world, but to have already reached, in thought and in the tendency of their desires, the assembly of those who are in heaven.

Now it is not right that the wing of virginity should, by its own nature, be weighed down upon the earth, but that it should soar upwards to heaven, to a pure atmosphere, and to the life which is akin to that of angels. Whence also they, first of all, after their call and departure hence, who have rightly and faithfully contended as virgins for Christ, bear away the prize of victory, being crowned by Him with the flowers of immortality. For, as soon as their souls have left the world, it is said that the angels meet them with much rejoicing, and conduct them to the very pastures already spoken of, to which also they were longing to come, contemplating them in imagination from afar, when, while they were yet dwelling in their bodies, they appeared to them divine.

Chapter III.—The Lot and Inheritance of Virginity.

Furthermore, when they have come hither, they see wonderful and glorious and blessed things of beauty, and such as cannot be spoken to men. They see there righteousness itself and prudence, and love itself, and truth and temperance, and other flowers and plants of wisdom, equally splendid, of which we here behold only the shadows and apparitions, as in dreams, and think that they consist of the actions of men, because there is no clear image of them here, but only dim copies, which themselves we see often when making dark copies of them. For never has any one seen with his eyes the greatness or the form or the beauty of righteousness itself, or of understanding, or of peace; but there, in Him whose name is I AM, they are seen perfect and clear, as they are. For there is a tree of temperance itself, and of love, and of understanding, as there are plants of the fruits which grow here—as of grapes, the pomegranate, and of apples; and so, too, the fruits of those trees are gathered and eaten, and do not perish and wither, but those who gather them grow to immortality and a likeness to God. Just as he from whom all are descended, before the fall and the blinding of his eyes, being in paradise, enjoyed its fruits, God appointing man to dress and to keep the plants of wisdom. For it was entrusted to the first Adam to cultivate those fruits. Now Jeremiah saw that these things exist specially in a certain place, removed to a great distance from our world, where, compassionating those who have fallen from that good state, he says: "Learn where is wisdom, where is strength, where is understanding; that thou may know also where is length of days, and life, where is the light of the eyes, and peace. Who hath found out her place? Or who hath come into her treasures?" The virgins having entered into the treasures of these things, gather the reasonable fruits of the virtues, sprinkled with manifold and well-ordered lights, which, like a fountain, God throws up over them, irradiating that state with unquenchable lights. And they sing harmoniously, giving glory to God. For a pure atmosphere is shed over them, and one which is not oppressed by the sun.

Chapter IV.—Exhortation to the Cultivation of Virginity; A Passage from the Apocalypse is Proposed to Be Examined.

Now, then, O Virgins, daughters of undefiled temperance, let us strive for a life of blessedness and the kingdom of heaven. And do ye unite with those before you in an earnest desire for the same glory of chastity, caring little for the things of this life. For immortality and chastity do not contribute a little to happiness, raising up the flesh aloft, and drying up its moisture and its clay-like weight, by a greater force of attraction. And let not the uncleanness which you hear creep in and weigh you down to the earth; nor let sorrow transform your joy, melting away your hopes in better things; but shake off incessantly the calamities which come upon you, not defiling your mind with lamentations. Let faith conquer wholly, and let its light drive away the visions of evil which crowd around the heart. For, as when the moon brightly shining fills the heaven with its light, and all the air becomes clear, but suddenly the clouds from the west, enviously rushing in, for a little while overshadow its light, but do not destroy it, since they are immediately driven away by a blast of the wind; so ye also, when causing the light of chastity to shine in the world, although pressed upon by afflictions and labors, do not grow weary and abandon your hopes. For the clouds which come from the Evil One are driven away by the Spirit, if ye, like your Mother, who gives birth to the male Virgin in heaven, fear nothing the serpent that lies in wait and plots against you; concerning whom I intend to discourse to you more plainly; for it is now time.

John, in the course of the Apocalypse, says: "And there appeared a great wonder in heaven; a woman clothed with the sun, and the moon under her feet, and upon her head a crown of twelve stars: and she, being with child, cried, travailing in birth, and pained to be delivered. And there appeared another wonder in heaven; and behold a great red dragon, having seven heads and ten horns, and seven crowns upon his heads. And his tail drew the third part of the stars of heaven, and did cast them to the earth: and the dragon stood before the woman which was ready to be delivered, for to devour her child as soon as it was born. And she brought forth a man-child, who was to rule all nations with a rod of iron: and her child was caught up unto God, and to His throne. And the woman fled into the wilderness, where she hath a place prepared of God, that they should feed her there a thousand two hundred and threescore days." So far we have given, in brief, the history of the woman and the dragon. But to search out and explain the solution of them is beyond my powers. Nevertheless, let me venture, trusting in Him who commanded to search the Scriptures. If, then, you agree with this, it will not be difficult to undertake it; for you will quite pardon me, if I am unable sufficiently to explain the exact meaning of the Scripture.

Chapter V.—The Woman Who Brings Forth, to Whom the Dragon is Opposed, the Church; Her Adornment and Grace.

The woman who appeared in heaven clothed with the sun, and crowned with twelve stars, and having the moon for her footstool, and being with child, and travailing in birth, is certainly, according to the accurate interpretation, our mother, O virgins, being a power by herself distinct from her children; whom the prophets, according to the aspect of their subjects, have called sometimes Jerusalem, sometimes a Bride, sometimes Mount Zion, and sometimes the Temple and Tabernacle of God. For she is the power which is desired to give light in the prophet, the Spirit crying to her: "Arise, shine; for thy light is come, and the glory of the Lord is risen upon thee. For, behold, the darkness shall cover the earth, and gross darkness the people: but the Lord shall arise upon thee, and His glory shall be seen upon thee. And the Gentiles shall come to thy light, and kings to the brightness of thy rising. Lift up thine eyes round about, and see; all they gather themselves together, they come to thee: thy sons shall come from far, and thy daughters shall be nursed at thy side." It is the Church whose children shall come to her with all speed after the resurrection, running to her from all quarters. She rejoices receiving the light which never goes down, and clothed with the brightness of the Word as with a robe. For with what other more precious or honorable ornament was it becoming that the queen should be adorned, to be led as a Bride to the Lord, when she had received a garment of light, and therefore was called by the Father? Come, then, let us go forward in our discourse, and look upon this marvelous woman as upon virgins prepared for a marriage, pure and undefiled, perfect and radiating a permanent beauty, wanting nothing of the brightness of light; and instead of a dress, clothed with light itself; and instead of precious stones, her head adorned with shining stars. For instead of the clothing which we have, she had light; and for gold and brilliant stones, she had stars; but stars not such as those which are set in the invisible heaven, but better and more resplendent, so that those may rather be considered as their images and likenesses.

Chapter VI.—The Works of the Church, the Bringing Forth of Children in Baptism; The Moon in Baptism, the Full Moon of Christ's Passion.

Now the statement that she stands upon the moon, as I consider, denotes the faith of those who are cleansed from corruption in the laver *of regeneration*, because the light of the moon has more resemblance to tepid water, and all moist substance is dependent upon her. The Church, then, stands upon our faith and adoption, under the figure of the moon, until the fullness of the nations come in, laboring and bringing forth natural men as spiritual men; for which reason too she is a mother. For just as a woman receiving the unformed seed of a man, within a certain time brings forth a perfect man, in the same way, one should say, does the Church conceive those who flee to the Word, and, forming them according to the likeness and form of Christ, after a certain time produce them as citizens of that blessed state. Whence it is necessary that she should stand upon the laver, bringing forth those who are washed in it. And in this way the power which she has in connection with the laver is called the moon, because the regenerate shine being renewed with a new ray, that is, a new light. Whence, also, they are by a descriptive term called newly-enlightened; the moon ever showing forth anew to them the spiritual full moon, namely, the period and the memorial of the passion, until the glory and the perfect light of the great day arise.

Chapter VII.—The Child of the Woman in the Apocalypse Not Christ, But the Faithful Who are Born in the Laver.

If anyone, for there is no difficulty in speaking distinctly, should be vexed, and reply to what we have said: "But how, O virgins, can this explanation seem to you to be according to the mind of Scripture, when the Apocalypse plainly defines that the Church brings forth a male, while you teach that her labor-pains have their fulfilment in those who are washed in the laver?" We will answer, But, O faultfinder, not even to you will it be possible to show that Christ Himself is the one who is born. For long before the Apocalypse, the mystery of the Incarnation of the Word was fulfilled. And John speaks concerning things present and things to come. But Christ, long ago conceived, was not caught up to the throne of God when He was brought forth, from fear of the serpent injuring Him. But for this was He begotten, and Himself came down from the throne of the Father, that He should remain and subdue the dragon who made an assault upon the flesh. So that you also must confess that the Church labors and gives birth to those who are baptized. As the spirit says somewhere in Isaiah: "Before she travailed, she brought forth; before her pain came, she was delivered of a man-child. Who hath heard such a thing? Who hath seen such things? Shall the earth be made to bring forth in one day? Or shall a nation be born at once? For as soon as Zion travailed, she brought forth her children." From whom did he flee? Surely from the dragon, that the spiritual Zion might bear a masculine people, who should come back from the passions and weakness of women to the unity of the Lord, and grow strong in manly virtue.

Chapter VIII.—The Faithful in Baptism Males, Configured to Christ; The Saints Themselves Christs.

Let us then go over the ground again from the beginning, until we come in course to the end, explaining what we have said. Consider if the passage seems to you to be explained to your mind. For I think that the Church is here said to give birth to a male; since the enlightened receive the features, and the image, and the manliness of Christ, the likeness of the form of the Word being stamped upon them, and begotten in them by a true knowledge and faith, so that in each one Christ is spiritually born. And, therefore, the Church swells and travails in birth until Christ is formed in us, so that each of the saints, by partaking of Christ, has been born a Christ. According to which meaning it is said in a certain scripture, "Touch not mine anointed, and do my prophets no harm," as though those who were baptized into Christ had been made Christs by communication of the Spirit, the Church contributing here their clearness and transformation into the image of the Word. And Paul confirms this, teaching it plainly, where he says: "For this cause I bow my knees unto the Father of our Lord Jesus Christ, of whom the whole family in heaven and earth is named, that He would grant you, according to the riches of His glory, to be strengthened with might by His Spirit in the inner man; that Christ may dwell in your hearts by faith." For it is necessary that the word of truth should be imprinted and stamped upon the souls of the regenerate.

Chapter IX.—The Son of God, Who Ever Is, is To-Day Begotten in the Minds and Sense of the Faithful.

Now, in perfect agreement and correspondence with what has been said, seems to be this which was spoken by the Father from above to Christ when He came to be baptized in the water of the Jordan, "Thou art my son: this day have I begotten thee;" for it is to be remarked that He was declared to be His Son unconditionally, and without regard to time; for He says

"Thou art," and not "Thou hast become," showing that He had neither recently attained to the relation of Son, nor again, having begun before, after this had an end, but having been previously begotten, that He was to be, and was the same. But the expression, "This day have I begotten thee," signifies that He willed that He who existed before the ages in heaven should be begotten on the earth—that is, that He who was before unknown should be made known. Now, certainly, Christ has never yet been born in those men who have never perceived the manifold wisdom of God—that is, has never been known, has never been manifested, has never appeared to them. But if these also should perceive the mystery of grace, then in them too, when they were converted and believed, He would be born in knowledge and understanding. Therefore from hence the Church is fitly said to form and beget the male Word in those who are cleansed. So far I have spoken according to my ability concerning the travail of the Church; and here we must change to the subject of the dragon and the other matters. Let us endeavor, then, to explain it in some measure, not deterred by the greatness of the obscurity of the Scripture; and if anything difficult comes to be considered, I will again help you to cross it like a river.

Chapter X.—The Dragon, the Devil; The Stars Struck from Heaven by the Tail of the Dragon, Heretics; The Numbers of the Trinity, that Is, the Persons Numbered; Errors Concerning Them.

The dragon, which is great, and red, and cunning, and manifold, and seven-headed, and horned, and draws down the third part of the stars, and stands ready to devour the child of the woman who is travailing, is the devil, who lies in wait to destroy the Christ-accepted mind of the baptized, and the image and clear features of the Word which had been brought forth in them. But he misses and fails of his prey, the regenerate being caught up on high to the throne of God—that is, the mind of those who are renovated is lifted up around the divine seat and the basis of truth against which there is no stumbling, being taught to look upon and regard the things which are there, so that it may not be deceived by the dragon weighing them down. For it is not allowed to him to destroy those whose thoughts and looks are upwards. And the stars, which the dragon touched with the end of his tail, and drew them down to earth, are the bodies of heresies; for we must say that the stars, which are dark, obscure, and falling, are the assemblies of the heterodox; since they, too, wish to be acquainted with the heavenly ones, and to have believed in Christ, and to have the seat of their soul in heaven, and to come near to the stars as children of light. But they are dragged down, being shaken out by the folds of the dragon, because they did not remain within the triangular forms of godliness, falling away from it with respect to an orthodox service. Whence also they are called the third part of the stars, as having gone astray with regard to one of the three Persons of the Trinity. As when they say, like Sabellios, that the Almighty Person of the Father Himself suffered; or as when they say, like Artemas, that the Person of the Son was born and manifested only in appearance; or when they contend, like the Ebionites, that the prophets spoke of the Person of the Spirit, of their own motion. For of Marcion and Valentinus, and those about Elkesaios and others, it is better not even to make mention.

Chapter XI.—The Woman with the Male Child in the Wilderness the Church; The Wilderness Belongs to Virgins and Saints; The Perfection of Numbers and Mysteries; The Equality and Perfection of the Number Six; The Number Six Related to Christ; From This Number, Too, the Creation and Harmony of the World Completed.

Now she who brings forth, and has brought forth, the masculine Word in the hearts of the faithful, and who passed, undefiled and uninjured by the wrath of the beast, into the wilderness, is, as we have explained, our mother the Church. And the wilderness into which she comes, and is nourished for a thousand two hundred and sixty days, which is truly waste and unfruitful of evils, and barren of corruption, and difficult of access and of transit to the multitude; but fruitful and abounding in pasture, and blooming and easy of access to the holy, and full of wisdom, and productive of life, is this most lovely, and beautifully wooded and well-watered abode of Arete. Here the south wind awakes, and the north wind blows, and the spices flow out, and all things are filled with refreshing dews, and crowned with the unfading plants of immortal life; in which we now gather flowers, and weave with sacred fingers the purple and glorious crown of virginity for the queen. For the Bride of the Word is adorned with the fruits of virtue. And the thousand two hundred and sixty days that we are staying here, O virgins, is the accurate and perfect understanding concerning the Father, and the Son, and the Spirit, in which our mother increases, and rejoices, and exults throughout this time, until the restitution of the new dispensation, when, coming into the assembly in the heavens, she will no longer contemplate the I AM through the means of *human* knowledge, but will clearly behold entering in together with Christ. For a thousand, consisting of a hundred multiplied by ten, embraces a full and perfect number, and is a symbol of the Father Himself, who made the universe by Himself, and rules all things for Himself. Two hundred embraces two perfect numbers united together, and is the symbol of the Holy Spirit, since He is the Author of our knowledge of the Son and the Father. But sixty has the number six multiplied by ten, and is a symbol of Christ, because the number six proceeding from unity is composed of its proper parts, so that nothing in it is wanting or redundant, and is complete when resolved into its parts. Thus it is necessary that the number six, when it is divided into even parts by even parts, should again make up the same quantity from its separated segments. For, first, if divided equally, it makes three; then, if divided into three parts, it makes two; and again, if divided by six, it makes one, and is again collected into itself. For when divided into twice three, and three times two, and six times one, when the three and the two and the one are put together, they complete the six again. But everything is of necessity perfect which neither needs anything else in order to its completion, nor has anything over. Of the other numbers, some are more than perfect, as twelve. For the half of it is six, and the third four, and the fourth three, and the sixth two, and the twelfth one. The numbers into which it can be divided, when put together, exceed twelve, this number not having preserved itself equal to its parts, like the number six. And those which are imperfect, are numbers like eight. For the half of it is four, and the fourth two, and the eighth one. Now the numbers into which it is divided, when put together, make seven, and one is wanting to its completion, not being in all points harmonious with itself, like six, which has reference to the Son of God, who came from the fullness of the Godhead into a human life. For having emptied Himself, and taken upon Him the form of a slave, He was restored again to His former perfection and dignity. For He being humbled, and apparently degraded, was restored again from His humiliation and degradation to His former completeness and greatness, having never been diminished from His essential perfection.

Moreover, it is evident that the creation of the world was accomplished in harmony with this number, God having made heaven and earth, and the things which are in them, in six days; the word of creative power containing the number six, in accordance with which the Trinity is the maker of bodies. For length, and breadth, and depth make up a body. And the number six is composed of triangles. On these subjects, however, there is not sufficient time at present to enlarge with accuracy, for fear of letting the main subject slip, in considering that which is secondary.

Chapter XII.—Virgins are Called to the Imitation of the Church in the Wilderness Overcoming the Dragon.

The Church, then, coming hither into this wilderness, a place unproductive of evils, is nourished, flying on the heavenward wings of virginity, which the Word called the "wings of great eagle," having conquered the serpent, and driven away from her full moon the wintry clouds. It is for the sake of these things, meanwhile, that all these discourses are held, teaching us, O fair virgins, to imitate according to our strength our mother, and not to be troubled by the pains and changes and afflictions of life, that you may enter in exulting with her into the bride-chamber, showing your lamps. Do not, therefore, lose courage on account of the schemes and slanders of the beast, but bravely prepare for the battle, armed with the helmet of salvation, and the breastplate, and the greaves. For you will bring upon him an immense consternation when you attack him with great advantage and courage; nor will he at all resist, seeing his adversaries set in array by One more powerful; but the many headed and many-faced beast will immediately allow you to carry off the spoils of the seven contests:—

"Lion in front, but dragon all behind,
And in the midst a she-goat breathing forth
Profuse the violence of flaming fire.
Her slew Bellerophon in truth. And this
Slew Christ the King; for many she destroyed,
Nor could they bear the fetid foam which burst
From out the fountain of her horrid jaws;"

unless Christ had first weakened and overcome her, making her powerless and contemptible before us.

Chapter XIII.—The Seven Crowns of the Beast to Be Taken Away by Victorious Chastity; The Ten Crowns of the Dragon, the Vices Opposed to the Decalogue; The Opinion of Fate the Greatest Evil.

Therefore, taking to you a masculine and sober mind, oppose your armor to the swelling beast, and do not at all give way, nor be troubled because of his fury. For you will have immense glory if you overcome him, and take away the seven crowns which are upon him, on account of which we have to struggle and wrestle, according to our teacher Paul. For she who having first overcome the devil, and destroyed his seven heads, becomes possessed of the seven crowns of virtue, having gone through the seven great struggles of chastity. For incontinence and luxury is a head of the dragon; and whoever bruises this is wreathed with the crown of temperance. Cowardice and weakness is also a head; and he who treads upon this carries off the crown of martyrdom. Unbelief and folly, and other similar fruits of wickedness, is another head; and he who has overcome these and destroyed them carries off the honors connected with them, the power of the dragon being in many ways rooted up. Moreover, the ten horns and stings which he was said to have upon his heads are the ten opposites, O virgins, to the Decalogue, by which he was accustomed to gore and cast down the souls of many imagining and contriving things in opposition to the law, "Thou shalt love the Lord thy God," and to the other precepts which follow. Consider now the fiery and bitter horn of fornication, by which he casts down the incontinent; consider adultery, consider falsehood, covetousness, theft, and the other sister and related vices, which flourish by nature around his murderous heads, which if you root out with the aid of Christ, you will receive, as it were, divine heads, and will bloom with the crowns gained from the dragon. For it is our duty to prefer and to set forward the best things, who have received, above the earth-born, a commanding and voluntary mind, and one free from all necessity, so as to make choice like masters of the things which please us, not being in bondage to fate or fortune. And so no man would be master of himself and good, unless selecting the human example of Christ, and bringing himself to the likeness of Him, he should imitate Him in his manner of life. For of all evils the greatest which is implanted in many is that which refers the causes of sins to the motions of the stars, and says that our life is guided by the necessities of fate, as those say who study the stars, with much insolence. For they, trusting more in guessing than in prudence, that is, in something between truth and falsehood, go far astray from the sight of things as they are. Whence, if you permit me, O Arete, now that I have completed the discourse which you, my mistress, appointed to be spoken, I will endeavor, with your assistance and favor, to examine carefully the position of those who are offended, and deny that we speak the truth, when we say that man is possessed of free-will, and prove that

> "They perish self-destroyed,
> By their own fault,"

choosing the pleasant in preference to the expedient.

Arete. I do permit you and assist you; for your discourse will be perfectly adorned when you have added this to it.

Chapter XIV.—The Doctrine of Mathematicians Not Wholly to Be Despised, When They are Concerned About the Knowledge of the Stars; The Twelve Signs of the Zodiac Mythical Names.

Thekla. Resuming then, let us first lay bare, in speaking of those things according to our power, the imposture of those who boast as though they alone had comprehended from what forms the heaven is arranged, in accordance with the hypothesis of the Chaldeans and Egyptians. For they say that the circumference of the world is likened to the turnings of a well-rounded globe, the earth having a central point. For its outline being spherical, it is necessary, they say, since there are the same distances of the parts, that the earth should be the center of the universe, around which, as being older, the heaven is whirling. For if a circumference is described from the central point, which seems to be a circle,—for it is impossible for a circle to be described without a point, and it is impossible for a circle to be without a point,—surely the earth consisted before all, they say, in a state of chaos and disorganization. Now certainly the wretched ones were overwhelmed in the chaos of error, "because that, when they knew God, they glorified Him not as God, neither were thankful; but became vain in their imaginations, and their foolish heart was darkened;" and their wise men said that nothing earth-born was more honorable or more ancient than the Olympians. Whence they are not mere children who know Christ, like the Greeks, who, burying the truth in fairies and fictions, rather than in artistic words, ascribing human calamities to the heavens, are not ashamed to describe the circumference of the world by geometrical theorems and figures, and explain that the heaven is adorned with the images of birds and of animals that live in water and on dry land, and that the qualities of the stars were made from the calamities of the men of old, so that the movements of the planets, in their opinion, depended upon the same kind of bodies. And they say that the stars revolve around the nature of the twelve signs of the Zodiac, being drawn along by the passage of the circle of the Zodiac, so that through their intermingling they see the things which happen to many, according to their conjunctions and departures, their rising and setting.

    For the whole heaven being spherical, and having the earth for its central point, as they think, because all the straight lines from the circumference falling upon the earth are equal to one another, holds back from the circles which surround it, of which the meridian is the greatest; and the second, which divides it into two equal parts, is the horizon; and the third, which separates these, the equinoctial; and on each side of this the two tropics, the summer and the winter—the one on the north, and the other on the south. Beyond is that which is called the axis, around which are the greater and lesser Bears, and beyond them is the tropic. And the Bears, turning about themselves, and weighing upon the axis, which passes through the poles, produce the motion of the whole world, having their heads against each other's loins, and being untouched by our horizon.

Then they say that the Zodiac touches all the circles, making its movements diagonally, and that there are in it a number of signs, which are called the twelve signs of the Zodiac, beginning with the Ram, and going on to the Fishes, which, they say, were so determined from mythical causes; saying that it was the Ram that conveyed Helle, the daughter of Athamas, and her brother Phryxos into Scythia; and that the head of the Ox is in honor of Zeus, who, in the form of a Bull, carried over Europe into Crete; and they say the circle called the Galaxy, or milky way, which reaches from the Fishes to the Ram, was poured forth for Herakles from the breasts of Hera, by the commands of Zeus. And thus, according to them, there was no natal destiny before Europe or Phryxos, and the Dioscuroi, and the other signs of the Zodiac, which were placed among the constellations, from men and beasts. But our ancestors lived without destiny. Let us endeavor now to crush falsehood, like physicians, taking its edge off, and quenching it with the healing medicine of words, here considering the truth.

Chapter XV.—Arguments from the Novelty of Fate and Generation; That Golden Age, Early Men; Solid Arguments Against the Mathematicians.

If it were better, O wretched ones, that man should be subject to *the star of* his birth, than that he should not, why was not his generation and birth from the very time when the race of man began to be? And if it was, what is the need of those which had lately been placed among the stars, of the Lion, the Crab, the Twins, the Virgin, the Bull, the Balance, the Scorpion, the Ram, the Archer, the Fishes, the Goat, the Watercarrier, Perseus, Cassiopeia, Cepheus, Pegasus, Hydra, the Raven, the Cup, the Lyre, the Dragon, and others, from which you introduce, by your instructions, many to the knowledge of mathematics, or, rather, to a knowledge which is anathema? Well, then, either there was generation among those before, and the removal of these *creatures above* was absurd; or else there was not, and God changed human life into a better state and government than that of those who before that lived an inferior life. But the ancients were better than those of the present time; whence theirs was called the golden age. There was then no natal destiny.

If the sun, driving through the circles and passing along the signs of the Zodiac in his annual periods, accomplishes the changes and turnings of the seasons, how did those who were born before the signs of the Zodiac were placed among the stars, and the heaven was adorned with them, continue to exist, when summer, autumn, winter, and spring, were not as yet separated from each other, by means of which the body is increased and strengthened? But they did exist, and were longer lived and stronger than those who live now, since God then disposed the seasons in the same manner. The heaven was not then diversified by such shapes.

If the sun and the moon and the other stars were made for the division and protection of the members of the time, and for the adornment of the heaven, and the changes of the seasons, they are divine, and better than men; for these must needs pass a better life, and a blessed and peaceful one, and one which far exceeds our own life in righteousness and virtue, observing a motion which is well-ordered and happy. But if they are the causes of the calamities and mischief of mortals, and busy themselves in working the lasciviousness, and the changes and vicissitudes of life, then they are more miserable than men, looking upon the earth, and their weak and lawless actions, and doing nothing better than men, if at least our life depends upon their revolutions and movements.

Chapter XVI.—Several Other Things Turned Against the Same Mathematicians.

If no action is performed without a previous desire, and there is no desire without a want, yet the Divine Being has no wants, and therefore has no conception of evil. And if the nature of the stars be nearer in order to that of God, being better than the virtue of the best men, then the stars also are neither productive of evil, nor in want.

And besides, every one of those who are persuaded that the sun and moon and stars are divine, will allow that they are far removed from evil, and incapable of human actions which spring from the sense of pleasure and pain; for such abominable desires are unsuitable to heavenly beings. But if they are by nature exempt from these, and in no want of anything, how should they be the causes to men of those things which they do not will themselves, and from which they are exempt?

Now those who decide that man is not possessed of free-will, and affirm that he is governed by the unavoidable necessities of fate, and her unwritten commands, are guilty of impiety towards God Himself, making Him out to be the cause and author of human evils. For if He harmoniously orders the whole circular motion of the stars, with a wisdom which man can neither express nor comprehend, directing the course of the universe; and the stars produce the qualities of virtue and vice in human life, dragging men to these things by the chains of necessity; then they declare God to be the Cause and Giver of evils. But God is the cause of injury to no one; therefore fate is not the cause of all things.

Whoever has the least intelligence will confess that God is good, righteous, wise, true, helpful, not the cause of evils, free from passion, and everything of that kind. And if the righteous be better than the unrighteous, and unrighteousness be abominable to them, God, being righteous, rejoices in righteousness, and unrighteousness is hateful to Him, being opposed and hostile to righteousness. Therefore God is not the author of unrighteousness.

If that which profits is altogether good, and temperance is profitable to one's house and life and friends, then temperance is good. And if temperance be in its nature good, and licentiousness be opposed to temperance, and that which is opposed to good be evil, then licentiousness is evil. And if licentiousness be in its nature evil, and out of licentiousness come adulteries, thefts, quarrels, and murders, then a licentious life is in its nature evil. But the Divine Being is not by nature implicated in evils. Therefore our birth is not the cause of these things.

If the temperate are better than the incontinent, and incontinence is abominable to them, and God rejoices in temperance, being free from the knowledge of passions, then incontinence is hateful also to God. Moreover, that the action which is in accordance with temperance, being a virtue, is better than that which is in accordance with incontinence, which is a vice, we may learn from kings and rulers, and commanders, and women, and children, and citizens, and masters, and servants, and pedagogues, and teachers; for each of these is useful to himself and to the public when he is temperate; but when he is licentious he is injurious to himself and to the public. And if there be any difference between a filthy man and a noble man, a licentious and a temperate; and if the character of the noble and the temperate be the better, and that of the opposite the worse; and if those of the better character be near to God and His friends, and those of the worse be far from Him and His enemies, those who believe in fate make no distinction between righteousness and unrighteousness, between filthiness and nobility, between licentiousness and temperance, which is a contradiction. For if good be opposed to evil, and unrighteousness be evil, and this be opposed to righteousness and righteousness be good, and good be hostile to evil, and evil be unlike to good, then righteousness is different from unrighteousness. And therefore God is not the cause of evils, nor does He rejoice in evils. Nor does reason commend them, being good. If, then, any are evil, they are evil in accordance with the wants *and desires* of their minds, and not by necessity.

"They perish self-destroyed,
By their own fault."

If destiny leads one on to kill a man, and to stain his hands with murder, and the law forbids this, punishing criminals, and by threats restrains the decrees of destiny, such as committing injustice, adultery, theft, poisoning, then the law is in opposition to destiny; for those things which destiny appointed the law prohibits, and those things which the law prohibits destiny compels men to do. Hence law is hostile to destiny. But if it be hostile, then lawgivers do not act in accordance with destiny; for by passing decrees in opposition to destiny they destroy destiny. Either, then, there is destiny and there was no need of laws; or there are laws and they are not in accordance with destiny. But it is impossible that anyone should be born or anything done apart from destiny; for they say it is not lawful for anyone even to move a finger apart from fate. And therefore it was in accordance with destiny that Minos and Dracon, and Lycurgus, and Solon, and Zaleukos were law-givers and appointed laws, prohibiting adulteries, murders, violence, rape, thefts, as things which neither existed nor took place in accordance with destiny. But if these things were in accordance with destiny, then the laws were not in accordance with destiny. For destiny itself would not be destroyed by itself, cancelling itself, and contending against itself; here appointing laws forbidding adultery and murders, and taking vengeance upon and punishing the wicked, and there producing murders and adulteries. But this is impossible: for nothing is alien and abhorrent to itself, and self-destructive, and at variance with itself. And, therefore, there is no destiny.

If everything in the world falls out in accordance with destiny, and nothing without it, then the law must needs be produced by destiny. But the law destroys destiny, teaching that virtue should be learnt, and diligently performed; and that vice should be avoided, and that it is produced by want of discipline. Therefore there is no destiny.

If destiny makes men to injure one another, and to be injured by one another, what need is there of laws? But if laws are made that they may check the sinful, God having a care for those who are injured, it were better that the evil should not act in accordance with Fate, than that they should be set right, after having acted. But God is good and wise, and does what is best. Therefore there is no fixed destiny. Either education and habit are the cause of sins, or the passions of the soul, and those desires which arise through the body. But whichever of these be the cause, God is not the cause. If it is better to be righteous than to be unrighteous, why is not man made so at once from his birth? But if afterwards he is tempered by instruction and laws, that he may become better, he is so tempered as possessing free-will, and not by nature evil. If the evil are evil in accordance with destiny, by the decrees of Providence, they are not blameworthy and deserving of the punishment which is inflicted by the laws, since they live according to their own nature, and are not capable of being changed.

And, again, if the good, living according to their own proper nature, are praiseworthy, their natal destiny being the cause of their goodness; yet the wicked, living according to their own proper nature, are not blamable in the eye of a righteous judge. For, if we must speak plainly, he who lives according to the nature which belongs to him, in no way sins. For he did not make himself thus, but Fate; and he lives according to its motion, being urged on by unavoidable necessity. Then no one is bad. But some men are bad: and vice is blameworthy, and hostile to God, as reason has shown. But virtue is lovable and praiseworthy, God having appointed a law for the punishment of the wicked. Therefore there is no Fate.

Chapter XVII.—The Lust of the Flesh and Spirit: Vice and Virtue.

But why do I draw out my discourse to such length, spending the time with arguments, having set forth the things which are most necessary for persuasion, and to gain approval for that which is expedient; and having made manifest to all, by a few words, the inconsistency of their trick, so that it is now possible even for a child to see and perceive their error; and that to do good or evil is in our own power, and not decided by the stars. For there are two motions in us, the lust of the flesh and that of the soul, differing from each other, whence they have received two names, that of virtue and that of vice. And we ought to obey the most noble and most useful leading of virtue, choosing the best in preference to the base. But enough on these points. I must come to the end of my discourse; for I fear, and am ashamed, after these discourses on chastity, that I should be obliged to introduce the opinions of men who study the heavens, or rather who study nonsense, who waste their life with mere conceits, passing it in nothing but fabulous figments. And now may these offerings of ours, composed from the words which are spoken by God, be acceptable to thee, O Arete, my mistress.

Euboulios. How bravely and magnificently, O Gregorion, has Thekla debated!

Gregorion. What, then, would you have said, if you had listened to herself, speaking fluently, and with easy expression, with much grace and pleasure? So that she was admired by everyone who attended, her language blossoming with words, as she set forth intelligently, and in fact picturesquely, the subjects on which she spoke, her countenance suffused with the blush of modesty; for she is altogether brilliant in body and soul.

Euboulios. Rightly do you say this, Gregorion, and none of these things is false; for I knew her wisdom also from other noble actions, and what sort of things she succeeded in speaking, giving proof of supreme love to Christ; and how glorious she often appeared in meeting the chief conflicts of the martyrs, procuring for herself a zeal equal to her courage, and a strength of body equal to the wisdom of her counsels.

Gregorion. Most truly do you also speak. But let us not waste time; for we shall often be able to discuss these and other subjects. But I must now first relate to you the discourses of the other virgins which followed, as I promised; and chiefly those of Tusiane and Domnina; for these still remain. When, then, Thekla ceased speaking these things, Theopatra said that Arete directed Tusiane to speak; and that she, smiling, passed before her and said.

Discourse IX.—Tusiane.
Chapter I.—Chastity the Chief Ornament of the True Tabernacle; Seven Days Appointed to the Jews for Celebrating the Feast of Tabernacles: What They Signify;

The Sum of This Septenary Uncertain; Not Clear to Any One When the Consummation of the World Will Be; Even Now the Fabric of the World Completed.

O Arete, thou dearest boast to the lovers of virginity, I also implore thee to afford me thine aid, lest I should be wanting in words, the subject having been so largely and variously handled. Wherefore I ask to be excused exordium and introductions, lest, whilst I delay in embellishments suitable to them, I depart from the subject: so glorious, and honorable, and renowned a thing is virginity.

God, when He appointed to the true Israelites the legal rite of the true feast of the tabernacles, directed, in Leviticus, how they should keep and do honor to the feast; above all things, saying that each one should adorn his tabernacle with chastity. I will add the words themselves of Scripture, from which, without any doubt, it will be shown how agreeable to God, and acceptable to Him, is this ordinance of virginity: "In the fifteenth day of the seventh month, when ye have gathered in the fruit of the land, ye shall keep a feast unto the Lord seven days: on the first day shall be a Sabbath, and on the eighth day shall be a Sabbath. And ye shall take you on the first day the boughs of goodly trees, branches of palm-trees, and the boughs of thick trees, and willows of the brook; and ye shall rejoice before the Lord your God seven days. And ye shall keep it a feast unto the Lord seven days in the year. It shall be a statute forever in your generations; ye shall celebrate it in the seventh month. Ye shall dwell in booths seven days; all that are Israelites born shall dwell in booths; that your generations may know that I made the children of Israel to dwell in booths, when I brought them out of Egypt: I am the Lord your God."

Here the Jews, fluttering about the bare letter of Scripture, like drones about the leaves of herbs, but not about flowers and fruits as the bee, fully believe that these words and ordinances were spoken concerning such a tabernacle as they erect; as if God delighted in those trivial adornments which they, preparing, fabricate from trees, not perceiving the wealth of good things to come; whereas these things, being like air and phantom shadows, foretell the resurrection and the putting up of our tabernacle that had fallen upon the earth, which at length, in the seventh thousand of years, resuming again immortal, we shall celebrate the great feast of true tabernacles in the new and indissoluble creation, the fruits of the earth having been gathered in, and men no longer begetting and begotten, but God resting from the works of creation.

For since in six days God made the heaven and the earth, and finished the whole world, and rested on the seventh day from all His works which He had made, and blessed the seventh day and sanctified it, so by a figure in the seventh month, when the fruits of the earth have been gathered in, we are commanded to keep the feast to the Lord, which signifies that, when this world shall be terminated at the seventh thousand years, when God shall have completed the world, He shall rejoice in us. For now to this time all things are created by His all-sufficient will and inconceivable power; the earth still yielding its fruits, and the waters being gathered together in their receptacles; and the light still severed from darkness, and the allotted number of men not yet being complete; and the sun arising to rule the day, and the moon the night; and four-footed creatures, and beasts, and creeping things arising from the earth, and winged creatures, and creatures that swim, from the water. Then, when the appointed times shall have been accomplished, and God shall have ceased to form this creation, in the seventh month, the great resurrection-day, it is commanded that the Feast of our Tabernacles shall be celebrated to the Lord, of which the things said in Leviticus are symbols and figures, which things, carefully investigating, we should consider the naked truth itself, for He says, "A wise man will hear, and will increase learning; and a man of understanding shall attain unto wise counsels: to understand a proverb, and the interpretation; the words of the wise, and their dark sayings."

Wherefore let it shame the Jews that they do not perceive the deep things of the Scriptures, thinking that nothing else than outward things are contained in the law and the prophets; for they, intent upon things earthly, have in greater esteem the riches of the world than the wealth which is of the soul. For since the Scriptures are in this way divided that some of them give the likeness of past events, some of them a type of the future, the miserable men, going back, deal with the figures of the future as if they were already things of the past. As in the instance of the immolation of the Lamb, the mystery of which they regard as solely in remembrance of the deliverance of their fathers from Egypt, when, although the firstborn of Egypt were smitten, they themselves were preserved by marking the door-posts of their houses with blood. Nor do they understand that by it also the death of Christ is personified, by whose blood souls made safe and sealed shall be preserved from wrath in the burning of the world; whilst the first-born, the sons of Satan, shall be destroyed with an utter destruction by the avenging angels, who shall reverence the seal of the Blood impressed upon the former.

Chapter II.—Figure, Image, Truth: Law, Grace, Glory; Man Created Immortal: Death Brought in by Destructive Sin.

And let these things be said for the sake of example, showing that the Jews have wonderfully fallen from the hope of future good, because they consider things present to be only signs of things already accomplished; whilst they do not perceive that the figures represent images, and images are the representatives of truth. For the law is indeed the figure and the shadow of an image, that is, of the Gospel; but the image, namely, the Gospel, is the representative of truth itself. For the men of olden time and the law foretold to us the characteristics of the Church, and the Church represents those of the new dispensation which is to come. Whence we, having received Christ, saying, "I am the truth," know that shadows and figures have ceased; and we hasten on to the truth, proclaiming its glorious images. For now we know "in part," and as it were "through a glass," since that which is perfect has not yet come to us; namely, the kingdom of heaven and the resurrection, when "that which is in part shall be done away." For then will all our tabernacles be firmly set up, when again the body shall rise, with bones again joined and compacted with flesh. Then shall we celebrate truly to the Lord a glad festal-day, when we shall receive eternal tabernacles, no more to perish or be dissolved into the dust of the tomb. Now, our tabernacle was at first fixed in an immoveable state, but was moved by transgression and bent to the earth, God putting an end to sin by means of death, lest man immortal, living a sinner, and sin living in him, should be liable to eternal curse. Wherefore he died, although he had not been created liable to death or corruption, and the soul was separated from the flesh, that sin might perish by death, not being able to live longer in one dead. Whence sin being dead and destroyed, again I shall rise immortal; and I praise God who by means of death frees His sons from death, and I celebrate lawfully to His honor a festal-day, adorning my tabernacle, that is my flesh, with good works, as there did the five virgins with the five-lighted lamps.

Chapter III.—How Each One Ought to Prepare Himself for the Future Resurrection.

In the first day of the resurrection I am examined whether I bring these things which are commanded, whether I am adorned with virtuous works, whether I am overshadowed by the boughs of chastity. For account the resurrection to be the erection of the tabernacle. Account that the things which are taken for the putting together of the tabernacle are the works of righteousness. I take, therefore, on the first day the things which are set down, that is, on the day in which I stand to be judged, whether I have adorned my tabernacle with the things commanded; if those things are found on that day which here in time we are commanded to prepare, and there to offer to God. But come, let us consider what follows.

"And ye shall take you," He says, "on the first day the boughs of goodly trees, branches of palm-trees, and the boughs of thick trees, and willows (and the tree of chastity) of the brook; and ye shall rejoice before the Lord your God." The Jews, uncircumcised in heart, think that the most beautiful fruit of wood is the citron wood, on account of its size; nor are they ashamed to say that God is worshipped with cedar, to whom not all the quadrupeds of the earth would suffice as a burnt-offering or as incense for burning. And moreover, O hard breasts, if the citron appear beautiful to you, why not the pomegranate, and other fruits of trees, and amongst them apples, which much surpass the citron? Indeed, in the Song of Songs, Solomon having made mention of all these fruits, passes over in silence the citron only. But this deceives the unwary, for they have not understood that the tree of life which Paradise once bore, now again the Church has produced for all, even the ripe and comely fruit of faith.

Such fruit it is necessary that we bring when we come to the judgment-seat of Christ, on the first day of the feast; for if we are without it we shall not be able to feast with God, nor to have part, according to John, in the first resurrection. For the tree of life is wisdom first begotten of all. "She is a tree of life to them that lay hold upon her," says the prophet; "and happy is every one that retained her." "A tree planted by the waterside, that will bring forth his fruit in due season;" that is, learning and charity and discretion are imparted in due time to those who come to the waters of redemption.

He that hath not believed in Christ, nor hath understood that He is the first principle and the tree of life, since he cannot show to God his tabernacle adorned with the most goodly of fruits, how shall he celebrate the feast? How shall he rejoice? Desires thou to know the goodly fruit of the tree? Consider the words of our Lord Jesus Christ, how pleasant they are beyond the children of men. Good fruit came by Moses, that is the Law, but not so goodly as the Gospel. For the Law is a kind of figure and shadow of things to come, but the Gospel is truth and the grace of life. Pleasant was the fruit of the prophets, but not so pleasant as the fruit of immortality which is plucked from the Gospel.

Chapter IV.—The Mind Clearer When Cleansed from Sin; The Ornaments of the Mind and the Order of Virtue; Charity Deep and Full; Chastity the Last Ornament of All; The Very Use of Matrimony to Be Restrained.

"And ye shall take you on the first day the boughs of goodly trees, branches of palm trees." This signifies the exercise of divine discipline, by which the mind that subdues the passions is cleansed and adorned by the sweeping out and ejection from it of sins. For it is necessary to come cleansed and adorned to the feast, arrayed, as by a decorator, in the discipline and exercise of virtue. For the mind being cleansed by laborious exercises from the distracting thoughts which darken it, quickly perceives the truth; as the widow in the Gospels found the piece of money after she had swept the house and cast out the dirt, that is, the passions which obscure and cloud the mind, which increase in us from our luxuriousness and carelessness.

Whoso, therefore, desires to come to that Feast of Tabernacles, to be numbered with the saints, let him first procure the goodly fruit of faith, then palm branches, that is, attentive meditation upon and study of the Scriptures, afterwards the far-spreading and thickly-leaved branches of charity, which He commands us to take after the palm branches; most fitly calling charity dense boughs, because it is all thick and close and very fruitful, not having anything bare or empty, but all full, both branches and trunks. Such is charity, having no part void or unfruitful.

For "though I sell all my goods and give to the poor, and though I yield up my body to the fire, and though I have so great faith that I can remove mountains, and have not charity, I am nothing." Charity, therefore, is a tree the thickest and most fruitful of all, full and abounding copiously abounding in graces.

After this, what else does He will that we should take? Willow branches; by that figure indicating righteousness, because "the just," according to the prophet, shall spring up "as grass in the midst of the waters, as willows by the watercourses," flourishing in the word. Lastly, to crown all, it is commanded that the bough of the Agnos tree be brought to decorate the Tabernacle, because it is by its very name the tree of chastity, by which those already named are adorned. Let the wanton now be gone, who, through their love of pleasure, reject chastity. How shall they enter into the feast with Christ who have not adorned their tabernacle with boughs of chastity, that God-making and blessed tree with which all who are hastening to that assembly and nuptial banquet ought to be begirt, and to cover their loins? For come, fair virgins, consider the Scripture itself, and its commands, how the Divine word has assumed chastity to be the crown of those virtues and duties that have been mentioned, showing how becoming and desirable it is for the resurrection, and that without it no one will obtain the promises which we who profess virginity supremely cultivate and offer to the Lord. They also possess it who live chastely with their wives, and do, as it were about the trunk, yield its lowly branches bearing chastity, not being able like us to reach its lofty and mighty boughs, or even to touch them; yet they, too, offer no less truly, although in a less degree, the branches of chastity. But those who are goaded on by their lusts, although they do not commit fornication, yet who, even in the things which are permitted with a lawful wife, through the heat of unsubdued concupiscence are excessive in embraces, how shall they celebrate the feast? How shall they rejoice, who have not adorned their tabernacle, that is their flesh, with the boughs of the Agnos, nor have listened to that which has been said, that "they that have wives be as though they had none?"

Chapter V.—The Mystery of the Tabernacles.

Wherefore, above all other things, I say to those who love contests, and who are strongminded, that without delay they should honor chastity, as a thing the most useful and glorious. For in the new and indissoluble creation, whoever shall not be found decorated with the boughs of chastity, shall neither obtain rest, because he has not fulfilled the command of God according to the law, nor shall he enter into the land of promise, because he has not previously celebrated the Feast of Tabernacles. For they only who have celebrated the Feast of Tabernacles come to the Holy Land, setting out from those dwellings which are called tabernacles, until they come to enter into the temple and city of God, advancing to a greater and more glorious joy, as the Jewish types indicate. For like as the Israelites, having left the borders of Egypt, first came to the Tabernacles, and from hence, having again set forth, came into the land of promise, so also do we. For I also, taking my journey, and going forth from the Egypt of this life, came first to the resurrection, which is the true Feast of the Tabernacles, and there having set up my tabernacle, adorned with the fruits of virtue, on the first day of the resurrection, which is the day of judgment, celebrate with Christ the millennium of rest, which is called the seventh day, even the true Sabbath. Then again from thence I, a follower of Jesus, "who hath entered into the heavens," as they also, after the rest of the Feast of Tabernacles, came into the land of promise, come into the heavens, not continuing to remain in tabernacles—that is, my body not remaining as it was before, but, after the space of a thousand years, changed from a human and corruptible form into angelic size and beauty, where at last we virgins, when the festival of the resurrection is consummated, shall pass from the wonderful place of the tabernacle to greater and better things, ascending into the very house of God above the heavens, as, says the Psalmist, "in the voice of praise and thanksgiving, among such as keep holy day." I, O Arete, my mistress, offer as a gift to thee this robe, adorned according to my ability.

Euboulios. I am much moved, O Gregorion, considering within myself in how great anxiety of mind Domnina must be from the character of the discourses, perplexed in heart as she is, and with good cause, fearing lest she should be at a loss for words, and should speak more feebly than the rest of the virgins, since they have spoken on the subject with such ability and variety. If, therefore, she was evidently moved, come and complete this too; for I wonder if she had anything to say, being the last speaker.

Gregorion. Theopatra told me, Euboulios, that she was greatly moved, but she was not perplexed from want of words. After, therefore, Tusiane had ceased, Arete looked at her and said, Come, my daughter, do thou also deliver a discourse, that our banquet may be quite complete. At this Domnina, blushing, and after a long delay, scarcely looking up, rose to pray, and turning round, invoked Wisdom to be her present helper. And when she had prayed, Theopatra said that suddenly courage came to her, and a certain divine confidence possessed her, and she said:—

Discourse X.—Domnina.
Chapter I.—Chastity Alone Aids and Effects the Most Praiseworthy Government of the Soul.

O Arete, I also, omitting the long preludes of exordiums, will endeavor according to my ability to enter upon the subject, lest, by delaying upon those matters which are outside the subject in hand, I should speak of them at greater length than their importance would warrant. For I account it a very great part of prudence not to make long speeches, which merely charm the ears, before coming to the main question, but to begin forthwith at the point in debate. So I will begin from thence, for it is time.

Nothing can so much profit a man, O fair virgins, with respect to moral excellence, as chastity; for chastity alone accomplishes and brings it about that the soul should be governed in the noblest and best way, and should be set free, pure from the stains and pollutions of the world. For which reason, when Christ taught us to cultivate it, and showed its unsurpassable beauty, the kingdom of the Evil One was destroyed, who aforetime led captive and enslaved the whole race of men, so that none of the more ancient people pleased the Lord, but all were overcome by errors, since the law was not of itself sufficient to free the human race from corruption, until virginity, succeeding the law, governed men by the precepts of Christ. Nor truly had the first men so often run headlong into combats and slaughter, into lust and idolatry, if the righteousness that is by the law had been to them sufficient for salvation. Now truly they were then confused by great and frequent calamities; but from the time when Christ was incarnate, and armed and adorned His flesh with virginity, the savage tyrant who was master of incontinence was taken away, and peace and faith have dominion, men no longer turning so much as before to idolatry.

Chapter II.—The Allegory of the Trees Demanding a King, in the Book of Judges, Explained.

But lest I should appear to some to be sophistical, and to conjecture these things from mere probabilities, and to babble, I will bring forward to you, O virgins, from the Old Testament, written prophecy from the Book of Judges, to show that I speak the truth, where the future reign of chastity was already clearly foretold. For we read: "The trees went forth on a time to anoint a king over them; and they said unto the olive-tree, Reign thou over us. But the olive-tree said unto them, Should I leave my fatness, wherewith by me they honor God and man, and go to be promoted over the trees? And the trees said to the fig-tree, Come thou, and reign over us. But the fig-tree said unto them, Should I forsake my sweetness, and my good fruit, and go to be promoted over the trees? Then said the trees unto the vine, Come thou, and reign over us. And the vine said unto them, Should I leave my wine, which cheered God and man, and go to be promoted over the trees? Then said all the trees unto the bramble, Come thou, and reign over us. And the bramble said unto the trees, If in truth ye anoint me king over you, then come and put your trust in my shadow; and if not, let fire come out of the bramble, and devour the cedars of Lebanon."

Now, that these things are not said of trees growing out of the earth, is clear. For inanimate trees cannot be assembled in council to choose a king, inasmuch as they firmly fixed by deep roots to the earth. But altogether are these things narrated concerning souls which, before the incarnation of Christ, too deeply luxuriating in transgressions, approach to God as suppliants, and ask His mercy, and that they may be governed by His pity and compassion, which Scripture expresses under the figure of the olive, because oil is of great advantage to our bodies, and takes away our fatigues and ailments, and affords light. For all lamp-light increases when nourished by oil. So also the mercies of God entirely dissolve death, and assist the human race, and nourish the light of the heart. And consider whether the laws, from the first created man until Christ in succession, were not set forth in these words by the Scripture by figments, in opposition to which the devil has deceived the human race. And it has likened the fig-tree to the command given to man in paradise, because, when he was deceived, he covered his nakedness with the leaves of a fig-tree; and the vine to the precept given to Noah at the time of the deluge, because, when overpowered by wine, he was mocked. The olive signifies the law given to Moses in the desert, because the prophetic grace, the holy oil, had failed from their inheritance when they broke the law. Lastly, the bramble not inaptly refers to the law which was given to the apostles for the salvation of the world; because by their instruction we have been taught virginity, of which alone the devil has not been able to make a deceptive image.

For which cause, also, four Gospels have been given, because God has four times given the Gospel to the human race, and has instructed them by four laws, the times of which are clearly known by the diversity of the fruits. For the fig-tree, on account of its sweetness and richness, represents the delights of man, which he had in paradise before the fall. Indeed, not rarely, as we shall afterwards show, the Holy Spirit takes the fruit of the fig-tree as an emblem of goodness. But the vine, on account of the gladness produced by wine, and the joy of those who were saved from wrath and from the deluge, signifies the change produced from fear and anxiety into joy. Moreover, the olive, on account of the oil which it produces, indicates the compassion of God, who again, after the deluge, bore patiently when men turned aside to ungodliness, so that He gave them the law and manifested Himself to some, and nourished by oil the light of virtue, now almost extinguished.

Chapter III.—The Bramble and the Agnos the Symbol of Chastity; The Four Gospels, that Is, Teachings or Laws, Instructing to Salvation.

Now the bramble commends chastity, for the bramble and the agnos is the same tree: by some it is called bramble, by others *agnos*. Perhaps it is because the plant is akin to virginity that it is called bramble and *agnos*; bramble, because of its strength and firmness against pleasures; agnos, because it always continues chaste. Hence the Scripture relates that Elijah, fleeing from the face of the woman Jezebel, at first came under a bramble, and there, having been heard, received strength and took food; signifying that to him who flies from the incitements of lust, and from a woman—that is, from pleasure—the tree of chastity is a refuge and a shade, ruling men from the coming of Christ, the chief of virgins. For when the first laws, which were published in the times of Adam and Noah and Moses, were unable to give salvation to man, the evangelical law alone has saved all.

And this is the cause why the fig-tree may be said not to have obtained the kingdom over trees, which, in a spiritual sense, mean men; and the fig-tree the command, because man desired, even after the fall, again to be subject to the dominion of virtue, and not to be deprived of the immortality of the paradise of pleasure. But, having transgressed, he was rejected and cast far away, as one who could no longer be governed by immortality, nor was capable of receiving it. And the first message to him after the transgression was preached by Noah, to which, if he had applied his mind, he might have been saved from sin; for in it he promised both happiness and rest from evils, if he gave heed to it with all his might, just as the vine promises to yield wine to those who cultivate it with care and labor. But neither did this law rule mankind, for men did not obey it, although zealously preached by Noah. But, after they began to be surrounded and drowning by the waters, they began to repent, and to promise that they would obey the commandments. Wherefore with scorn they are rejected as subjects; that is, they are contemptuously told that they cannot be helped by the law; the Spirit answering them back and reproaching them because they had deserted those men whom God had commanded to help them, and to save them, and make them glad; such as Noah and those with him. "Even to you, O rebellious," said he, "I come, to bring help to you who are destitute of prudence, and who differ in nothing from dry trees, and who formerly did not believe me when I preached that you ought to flee from present things."

Chapter IV.—The Law Useless for Salvation; The Last Law of Chastity Under the Figure of the Bramble.

And so those men, having been thus rejected from the divine care, and the human race having again given themselves up to error, again God sent forth, by Moses, a law to rule them and recall them to righteousness. But these, thinking fit to bid a long farewell to this law, turned to idolatry. Hence God gave them up to mutual slaughters, to exiles, and captivities, the law itself confessing, as it were, that it could not save them. Therefore, worn out with ills and afflicted, they again promised that they would obey the commandments; until God, pitying man the fourth time, sent chastity to rule over them, which Scripture consequently called the bramble. And she consuming pleasures threatens besides, that unless all undoubtingly obey her, and truly come to her, she will destroy all with fire, since there will be hereafter no other law or doctrine but judgment and fire. For this reason, man henceforth began to do righteousness, and firmly to believe in God, and to separate himself from the devil. Thus chastity was sent down, as being most useful and helpful to men. For of her alone was the devil unable to forge an imitation to lead men astray, as is the case with the other precepts.

Chapter V.—The Malignity of the Devil as an Imitator in All Things; Two Kinds of Fig- Trees and Vines.

The fig-tree, as I said, from the sweetness and excellence of its fruit, being taken as a type of the delights of paradise, the devil, having beguiled the man by its imitations, led him captive, persuading him to conceal the nakedness of his body by fig-leaves; that is, by their friction he excited him to sexual pleasure. Again, those that had been saved from the deluge, he intoxicated with a drink which was an imitation of the vine of spiritual joy; and again he mocked them, having stripped them of virtue. And what I say will hereafter be clearer.

The enemy, by his power, always imitates the forms of virtue and righteousness, not for the purpose of truly promoting its exercise, but for deception and hypocrisy. For in order that those who fly from death he may entice to death, he is outwardly dyed with the colors of immortality. And hence he wishes to seem a fig-tree or vine, and to produce sweetness and joy, and is "transformed into an angel of light," ensnaring many by the appearance of piety.

For we find in the Sacred Writings that there are two kinds of fig-trees and vines, "the good figs, very good; and the evil, very evil;" "wine that makes glad the heart of man," and wine which is the poison of dragons, and the incurable venom of asps. But from the time when chastity began to rule over men, the fraud was detected and overcome, Christ, the chief of virgins, overturning it. So both the true fig-tree and the true vine yield fruit after that the power of chastity has laid hold upon all men, as Joel the prophet preaches, saying: "Fear not, O land; be glad and rejoice, for the Lord will do great things. Be not afraid, ye beasts of the field; for the pastures of the wilderness do spring, for the tree bears her fruit, the fig-tree and the vine do yield their strength. Be glad then, ye children of Zion, and rejoice in the Lord your God, for He hath given you food unto righteousness;" calling the former laws the vine and the fig, trees bearing fruit unto righteousness for the children of the spiritual Zion, which bore fruit after the incarnation of the Word, when chastity ruled over us, when formerly, on account of sin and much error, they had checked and destroyed their buds. For the true vine and the true fig-tree were not able to yield such nourishment to us as would be profitable for life, whilst as yet the false fig-tree, variously adorned for the purpose of fraud, flourished. But when the Lord dried up the false branches, the imitations of the true branches, uttering the sentence against the bitter fig-tree, "Let no fruit grow on thee henceforward forever," then those which were truly fruit-bearing trees flourished and yielded food unto righteousness.

The vine, and that not in a few places, refers to the Lord Himself, and the fig-tree to the Holy Spirit, as the Lord "makes glad the hearts of men," and the Spirit heals them. And therefore Hezekiah is commanded first to make a plaster with a lump of figs—that is, the fruit of the Spirit—that he may be healed—that is, according to the apostle—by love; for he says, "The fruit of the Spirit is love, joy, peace, long-suffering, gentleness, goodness, faith, meekness, temperance;" which, on account of their great pleasantness, the prophet calls figs. Micah also says, "They shall sit every man under his vine and under his fig-tree; and none shall make them afraid." Now it is certain that those who have taken refuge and rested under the Spirit, and under the shadow of the Word, shall not be alarmed, nor frightened by him who troubles the hearts of men.

Chapter VI.—The Mystery of the Vision of Zechariah.

Moreover, Zechariah shows that the olive shadows forth the Law of Moses, speaking thus: "And the angel that talked with me came again and waked me, as a man that is wakened out of his sleep, and said unto me, what sees thou? And I said, I have looked, and behold a candlestick all of gold, with a bowl upon the top of it....And two olive-trees by it, one upon the right side of the bowl, and the other upon the left side thereof." And after a few words, the prophet, asking what are the olives on the right and left of the candlestick, and what the two olive-boughs in the hands of the two pipes, the angel answered and said: "These are the two sons of fruitfulness which stand by the Lord of the whole earth," signifying the two first-born virtues that are waiting upon God, which, in His dwelling, supply around the wick, through the boughs, the spiritual oil of God, that man may have the light of divine knowledge. But the two boughs of the two olives are the law and the prophets, around, as it were, the lot of the inheritance, of which Christ and the Holy Spirit are the authors, we ourselves meanwhile not being able to take the whole fruit and the greatness of these plants, before chastity began to rule the world, but only their boughs—to wit, the law and the prophets—did we formerly cultivate, and those moderately, often letting them slip. For who was ever able to receive Christ or the Spirit, unless he first purified himself? For the exercise which prepares the soul from childhood for desirable and delectable glory, and carries this grace safely thither with ease, and from small toils raises up mighty hopes, is chastity, which gives immortality to our bodies; which it becomes all men willingly to prefer in honor and to praise above all things; some, that by its means they may be betrothed to the Word, practicing virginity; and others, that by it they may be freed from the curse, "Dust thou art, and unto dust shalt thou return."

This, O Arete, is the discourse on virginity which you required of me, accomplished according to my ability; which I pray, O mistress, although it is mediocre and short, that thou wilt receive with kindness from me who was chosen to speak last.

Discourse XI.—Arete.

Chapter I.—The True and Chaste Virgins Few; Chastity a Contest; Thekla Chief of Virgins.

I do accept it, Theopatra related that Arete said, and approve of it all. For it is an excellent thing, even although you had not spoken so clearly, to take up and go through with earnestness those things which have been said, not to prepare a sweet entertainment for those who listen, but for correction, recollection, and abstinence. For whoever teaches that chastity is to be preferred and embraced first of all among my pursuits, rightly advises; which many think that they honor and cultivate, but which few, so to speak, really honor. For it is not one who has studied to restrain his flesh from the pleasure of carnal delight that cultivates chastity, if he do not keep in check the rest of the desires; but rather he dishonors it, and that in no small degree, by base lusts, exchanging pleasures for pleasures. Nor if he have strongly resisted the desires of the senses, but is lifted up with vainglory, and from this cause is able to repress the heats of burning lust, and reckon them all as nothing, can he be thought to honor chastity; for he dishonors it in that he is lifted up with pride, cleansing the outside of the cup and platter, that is, the flesh and the body, but injuring the heart by conceit and ambition. Nor when any one is conceited of riches is he desirous of honoring chastity; he dishonors it more than all, preferring a little gain to that to which nothing is comparable of those things that are in this life esteemed. For all riches and gold "in respect of it are as a little sand." And neither does he who loves himself above measure, and eagerly considers that which is expedient for himself alone, regardless of the necessities of his neighbor, honor chastity, but he also dishonors it. For he who has repelled from himself charity, mercy, and humanity, is much inferior to those who honorably exercise chastity. Nor is it right, on the one hand, by the use of chastity to keep virginity, and, on the other hand, to pollute the soul by evil deeds and lust; nor here to profess purity and continence, and there to pollute it by indulgence in vices. Nor, again, here to declare that the things of this world bring no care to himself; there to be eager in procuring them, and in concern about them. But all the members are to be preserved intact and free from corruption; not only those which are sexual, but those members also which minister to the service of lusts. For it would be ridiculous to preserve the organs of generation pure, but not the tongue; or to preserve the tongue, but neither the eyesight, the ears, nor the hands; or lastly, to preserve these pure, but not the mind, defiling it with pride and anger.

It is altogether necessary for him who has resolved that he will not err from the practice of chastity, to keep all his members and senses clean and under restraint, as is customary with the planks of ships, whose fastenings the ship-masters diligently join together, lest by any means the way and access may lie open for sin to pour itself into the mind. For great pursuits are liable to great falls, and evil is more opposed to that which is really good than to that which is not good. For many who thought that to repress vehement lascivious desires constituted chastity, neglecting other duties connected with it, failed also in this, and have brought blame upon those endeavoring after it by the right way, as you have proved who are a model in everything, leading a virgin life in deed and word. And now what that is which becomes a virgin state has been described.

And you all in my hearing having sufficiently contended in speaking, I pronounce victors and crown; but Thekla with a larger and thicker chaplet, as the chief of you, and as having shone with greater luster than the rest.

Chapter II.—Thekla Singing Decorously a Hymn, the Rest of the Virgins Sing with Her; John the Baptist a Martyr to Chastity; The Church the Spouse of God, Pure and Virgin.

Theopatra said that Arete having said these things, commanded them all to rise, and, standing under the Agnos, to send up to the Lord in a becoming manner a hymn of thanksgiving; and that Thekla should begin and should lead the rest. And when they had stood up, she said that Thekla, standing in the midst of the virgins on the right of Arete, decorously sang; but the rest, standing together in a circle after the manner of a chorus, responded to her: "I keep myself pure for Thee, O Bridegroom, and holding a lighted torch I go to meet Thee."

Thekla. 1. From above, O virgins, the sound of a noise that wakes the dead has come, bidding us all to meet the Bridegroom in white robes, and with torches towards the east. Arise, before the King enters within the gates.

Chorus. I keep myself pure for Thee, O Bridegroom, and holding a lighted torch I go to meet Thee.

Thekla. 2. Fleeing from the sorrowful happiness of mortals, and having despised the luxuriant delights of life and its love, I desire to be protected under Thy life-giving arms, and to behold Thy beauty forever, O blessed One.

Chorus. I keep myself pure for Thee, O Bridegroom, and holding a lighted torch I go to meet Thee.

Thekla. 3. Leaving marriage and the beds of mortals and my golden home for Thee, O King, I have come in undefiled robes, in order that I might enter with Thee within Thy happy bridal chamber.

Chorus. I keep myself pure for Thee, O Bridegroom, and holding a lighted torch I go to meet Thee.

Thekla. 4. Having escaped, O blessed One, from the innumerable enchanting wiles of the serpent, and, moreover, from the flame of fire, and from the mortal-destroying assaults of wild beasts, I await Thee from heaven.

Chorus. I keep myself pure for Thee, O Bridegroom, and holding a lighted torch I go to meet Thee.

Thekla. 5. I forget my own country, O Lord, through desire of Thy grace. I forget, also, the company of virgins, my fellows, the desire even of mother and of kindred, for Thou, O Christ, art all things to me.

Chorus. I keep myself pure for Thee, O Bridegroom, and holding a lighted torch I go to meet Thee.

Thekla. 6. Giver of life art Thou, O Christ. Hail, light that never sets, receive this praise.

The company of virgins call upon Thee, Perfect Flower, Love, Joy, Prudence, Wisdom, Word.

Chorus. I keep myself pure for Thee, O Bridegroom, and holding a lighted torch I go to meet Thee.

Thekla. 7. With open gates, O beauteously adorned Queen, admit us within thy chambers.

O spotless, gloriously triumphant Bride, breathing beauty, we stand by Christ, robed as He is, celebrating thy happy nuptials, O youthful maiden.

Chorus. I keep myself pure for Thee, O Bridegroom, and holding a lighted torch I go to meet Thee.

Thekla. 8. The virgins standing without the chamber, with bitter tears and deep moans, wail and mournfully lament that their lamps are gone out, having failed to enter in due time the chamber of joy.

Chorus. I keep myself pure for Thee, O Bridegroom, and holding a lighted torch I go to meet Thee.

Thekla. 9. For turning from the sacred way of life, unhappy ones, they have neglected to prepare sufficiency of oil for the path of life; bearing lamps whose bright light is dead, they groan from the inward recesses of their mind.

Chorus. I keep myself pure for Thee, O Bridegroom, and holding a lighted torch I go to meet Thee.

Thekla. 10. Here are cups full of sweet nectar; let us drink, O virgins, for it is celestial drink, which the Bridegroom hath placed for those duly called to the wedding.

Chorus. I keep myself pure for Thee, O Bridegroom, and holding a lighted torch I go to meet Thee.

Thekla. 11. Abel, clearly prefiguring Thy death, O blessed One, with flowing blood, and eyes lifted up to heaven, said, Cruelly slain by a brother's hand, O Word, I pray Thee to receive me.

Chorus. I keep myself pure for Thee, O Bridegroom, and holding a lighted torch I go to meet Thee.

Thekla. 12. Thy valiant son Joseph, O Word, won the greatest prize of virginity, when a woman heated with desire forcibly drew him to an unlawful bed; but he giving no heed to her fled stripped, and crying aloud:—

Chorus. I keep myself pure for Thee, O Bridegroom, and holding a lighted torch I go to meet Thee.

Thekla. 13. Jephthah offered his fresh slaughtered virgin daughter a sacrifice to God, like a lamb; and she, nobly fulfilling the type of Thy body, O blessed One, bravely cried:—

Chorus. I keep myself pure for Thee, O Bridegroom, and holding a lighted torch I go to meet Thee.

Thekla. 14. Daring Judith, by clever wiles having cut off the head of the leader of the foreign hosts, whom previously she had allured by her beautiful form, without polluting the limbs of her body, with a victor's shout said:—

The Writings of Methodius

Chorus. I keep myself pure for Thee, O Bridegroom, and holding a lighted torch I go to meet Thee.

Thekla. 15. Seeing the great beauty of Susanna, the two Judges, maddened with desire, said, O dear lady, we have come desiring secret intercourse with thee; but she with tremulous cries said:—

Chorus. I keep myself pure for Thee, O Bridegroom, and holding a lighted torch I go to meet Thee.

Thekla. 16. It is far better for me to die than to betray my nuptials to you, O mad for women, and so to suffer the eternal justice of God in fiery vengeance. Save me now, O Christ, from these evils.

Chorus. I keep myself pure for Thee, O Bridegroom, and holding a lighted torch I go to meet Thee.

Thekla. 17. Thy Precursor, washing multitudes of men in flowing lustral water, unjustly by a wicked man, on account of his chastity, was led to slaughter; but as he stained the dust with his life-blood, he cried to Thee, O blessed One:—

Chorus. I keep myself pure for Thee, O Bridegroom, and holding a lighted torch I go to meet Thee.

Thekla. 18. The parent of Thy life, that unspotted Grace and undefiled Virgin, bearing in her womb without the ministry of man, by an immaculate conception, and who thus became suspected of having betrayed the marriage-bed, she, O blessed One, when pregnant, thus spoke:—

Chorus. I keep myself pure for Thee, O Bridegroom, and holding a lighted torch I go to meet Thee.

Thekla. 19. Wishing to see Thy nuptial day, O blessed One, as many angels as Thou, O King, called from above, bearing the best gifts to Thee, came in unsullied robes:—

Chorus. I keep myself pure for Thee, O Bridegroom, and holding a lighted torch I go to meet Thee.

Thekla. 20. In hymns, O blessed spouse of God, we attendants of the Bride honor Thee, O undefiled virgin Church of snow-white form, dark haired, chaste, spotless, beloved.

Chorus. I keep myself pure for Thee, O Bridegroom, and holding a lighted torch I go to meet Thee.

Thekla. 21. Corruption has fled, and the tearful pains of diseases; death has been taken away, all folly has perished, consuming mental grief is no more; for again the grace of the God-Christ has suddenly shone upon mortals.

Chorus. I keep myself pure for Thee, O Bridegroom, and holding a lighted torch I go to meet Thee.

Thekla. 22. Paradise is no longer bereft of mortals, for by divine decree he no longer dwells there as formerly, thrust out from thence when he was free from corruption, and from fear by the various wiles of the serpents, O blessed One.

Chorus. I keep myself pure for Thee, O Bridegroom, and holding a lighted torch I go to meet Thee.

Thekla. 23. Singing the new song, now the company of virgins attends thee towards the heavens, O Queen, all manifestly crowned with white lilies, and bearing in their hands bright lights.

Chorus. I keep myself pure for Thee, O Bridegroom, and holding a lighted torch I go to meet Thee.

Thekla. 24. O blessed One, who inhabited the undefiled seats of heaven without beginning, who governed all things by everlasting power, O Father, with Thy Son, we are here, receive us also within the gates of life.

Chorus. I keep myself pure for Thee, O Bridegroom, and holding a lighted torch I go to meet Thee.

Chapter III.—Which are the Better, the Continent, or Those Who Delight in Tranquility of Life? Contests the Peril of Chastity: the Felicity of Tranquility; Purified and Tranquil Minds Gods: They Who Shall See God; Virtue Disciplined by Temptations.

Euboulios. Deservedly, O Gregorion, has Thekla borne off the chief prize.

Gregorion. Deservedly indeed.

Euboulios. But what about the stranger Telmisiake? Tell me, was she not listening from without? I wonder if she could keep silence on hearing of this banquet, and would not forthwith, as a bird flies to its food, listen to the things which were spoken.

Gregorion. The report is that she was present with Methodios when he inquired respecting these things of Arete. But it is a good as well as a happy thing to have such a mistress and guide as Arete, that is virtue.

Euboulios. But, Gregorion, which shall we say are the better, those who without lust govern concupiscence, or those who under the assaults of concupiscence continue pure?

Gregorion. For my part, I think those who are free from lust, for they have their mind undefiled, and are altogether uncorrupted, sinning in no respect.

Euboulios. Well, I swear by chastity, and wisely, O Gregorion. But lest in any wise I hinder you, if I gainsay your words, it is that I may the better learn, and that no one hereafter may refute me.

Gregorion. Gainsay me as you will, you have my permission. For, Euboulios, I think that I know sufficient to teach you that he who is not concupiscent is better than he who is. If I cannot, then there is no one who can convince you.

Euboulios. Bless me! I am glad that you answer me so magnanimously, and show how wealthy you are as regards wisdom.

Gregorion. A mere chatterer, so you seem to be, O Euboulios.

Euboulios. Why so?

Gregorion. Because you ask rather for the sake of amusement than of truth.

Euboulios. Speak fair, I pray you, my good friend; for I greatly admire your wisdom and renown. I say this because, with reference to the things that many wise men often dispute among themselves, you say that you not only understand them, but also vaunt that you can teach another.

Gregorion. Now tell me truly whether it is a difficulty with you to receive the opinion, that they who are not concupiscent excel those who are concupiscent, and yet restrain themselves? Or are you joking?

Euboulios. How so, when I tell you that I do not know? But, come, tell me, O wisest lady, in what do the non-concupiscent and chaste excel the concupiscent who live chastely?

Gregorion. Because, in the first place, they have the soul itself pure, and the Holy Spirit always dwells in it, seeing that it is not distracted and disturbed by fancies and unrestrained thoughts, so as to pollute the mind. But they are in every way inaccessible to lust, both as to their flesh and to their heart, enjoying tranquility from passions. But they who are allured from without, through the sense of sight, with fancies, and receiving lust flowing like a stream into the heart, are often not less polluted, even when they think that they contend and fight against pleasures, being vanquished in their mind.

Euboulios. Shall we then say that they who serenely live and are not disturbed by lusts are pure?

Gregorion. Certainly. For these are they whom God makes gods in the beatitudes; they who believe in Him without doubt. And He says that they shall look upon God with confidence, because they bring in nothing that darkens or confuses the eye of the soul for the beholding of God; but all desire of things secular being eliminated, they not only, as I said, preserve the flesh pure from carnal connection, but even the heart, in which, especially, as in a temple, the Holy Spirit rests and dwells, is open to no unclean thoughts.

Euboulios. Stay now; for I think that from hence we shall the better go on to the discovery of what things are truly the best; and, tell me, do you call anyone a good pilot?

Gregorion. I certainly do.

Euboulios. Whether is it he that saves his vessel in great and perplexing storms, or is it he who does so in a breathless calm?

Gregorion. He that does so in a great and perplexing storm.

Euboulios. Shall we not then say that the soul, which is deluged with the surging waves of the passions, and yet does not, on that account, weary or grow faint, but direct her vessel—that is, the flesh—nobly into the port of chastity, is better and more estimable than he that navigates in calm weather?

Gregorion. We will say so.

Euboulios. For to be prepared against the entrance of the gales of the Evil Spirit, and not to be cast away or overcome, but to refer all to Christ, and strongly to contend against pleasures, brings greater praise than he wins who lives a virgin life calmly and with ease.

Gregorion. It appears so.

Euboulios. And what says the Lord? Does He not seem to show that he who retains continence, though concupiscent, excels him who, having no concupiscence, leads a virgin life?

Gregorion. Where does He say so?

Euboulios. Where, comparing a wise man to a house well founded, He declares him immoveable because he cannot be overthrown by rains, and floods, and winds; likening, as it would seem, these storms to lusts, but the immoveable and unshaken firmness of the soul in chastity to the rock.

Gregorion. You appear to speak what is true.

Euboulios. And what say you of the physician? Do you not call him the best who has been proved in great diseases, and has healed many patients?

Gregorion. I do.

Euboulios. But the one who has never at any time practiced, nor ever had the sick in his hands, is he not still in all respects the inferior?

Gregorion. Yes.

Euboulios. Then we may certainly say that a soul which is contained by a concupiscent body, and which appeases with the medicaments of temperance the disorders arising from the heat of lusts, carries off the palm for healing, over one to whose lot it has fallen to govern aright a body which is free from lust.

Gregorion. It must be allowed.

Euboulios. And how is it in wrestling? Whether is the better wrestler he who has many and strong antagonists, and continually is contending without being worsted, or he who has no opponents?

Gregorion. Manifestly he who wrestles.

Euboulios. And, in wrestling, is not the athlete who contends the more experienced?

Gregorion. It must be granted.

Euboulios. Therefore it is clear that he whose soul contends against the impulses of lust, and is not borne down by it, but draws back and sets himself in array against it, appears stronger than he who does not lust.

Gregorion. True.

Euboulios. What then? Does it not appear to you, Gregorion, that there is more courage in being valiant against the assaults of base desires?

Gregorion. Yes, indeed.

Euboulios. Is not this courage the strength of virtue?

Gregorion. Plainly so.

Euboulios. Therefore, if endurance be the strength of virtue, is not the soul, which is troubled by lusts, and yet perseveres against them, stronger than that which is not so troubled?

Gregorion. Yes.

Euboulios. And if stronger, then better?

Gregorion. Truly.

Euboulios. Therefore the soul which is concupiscent, and exercises self-control, as appears from what has been said, is better than that which is not concupiscent, and exercises self-control.

Gregorion. You speak truly, and I shall desire still more fully to discourse with you concerning these things. If, therefore, it pleases you, tomorrow I will come again to hear respecting them. Now, however, as you see, it is time to betake ourselves to the care of the outward man.

Elucidations.

I.

(We here behold only shadows, etc.,)

Schleiermacher, in commenting on Plato's *Symposium*, remarks: "Even natural birth (i.e., in Plato's system) was nothing but a reproduction of the same *eternal form and idea*....The whole discussion displays the gradation, not only from that pleasure which arises from the contemplation of personal beauty through that which every larger object, whether single or manifold, may occasion, to that immediate pleasure of which the source is in the Eternal Beauty," etc. Our author ennobles such theorizing by mounting up to the great I Am.

II.

(Christ Himself is the one who is born)

Wordsworth, and many others of the learned, sustain our author's comment on this passage. So Aquinas, *ad loc.*, Bede, and many others. Methodius is incorrectly represented as *rejecting* the idea that "the woman" is the Blessed Virgin Mary, for no such idea existed for him to reject. He rejects the idea that the man-child is Christ; but that idea was connected with the supposition that the woman was the Church of the Hebrews bringing forth the Messiah. Gregory the Great regards the woman as the Christian Church. So Hippolytus: "By the woman…is meant most manifestly the Church, endued with the Father's Word, whose brightness is above the sun," etc. Bossuet says candidly, "C'est l'Église, tout éclatante de la lumière de J. C.," etc.

Now, note the progress of corruption, one fable engendering another. The text of Gen. iii. 15, contrary to the Hebrew, the Seventy, the Syriac, and the Vulgate itself, in the best mss., is made to read, "*She* shall bruise thy head," etc. The "woman," therefore, becomes the Mother of our Lord, and the "great red dragon" (of verse 3), from which the woman "fled into the wilderness," is next represented as *under her feet* (where the moon appears in the sacred narrative); and then the Immaculate Conception of her Holy Seed is transferred back to the mother of Mary, who is indecently discussed, and affirmed to have been blest with an "Immaculate Conception" when, in the ordinary process of nature, she was made the mother of the Virgin. So, then, the bull *Ineffabilis*—comes forth, eighteen hundred years after the event, with the announcement that what thousands of saints and many bishops of Rome have denounced as a fable must be received by all Christians on peril of eternal damnation. The worst of it all is the fact, that, as the mystery of the Incarnation of the Son of God has heretofore been the only "Immaculate Conception" known to the faith of Christendom, thousands now imagine that *this* is what was only so lately set forth, and what we must therefore renounce as false.

Concerning Free-Will.

Orthodoxus. The old man of Ithaca, according to the legend of the Greeks, when he wished to hear the song of the Sirens, on account of the charm of their voluptuous voice, sailed to Sicily in bonds, and stopped up the ears of his companions; not that he grudged them the hearing, or desired to load himself with bonds, but because the consequence of those singers' music to those who heard it was death. For such, in the opinion of the Greeks, are the charms of the Sirens. Now I am not within hearing of any such song as this; nor have I any desire to hear the Sirens who chant men's dirges, and whose silence is more profitable to men than their voice; but I pray to enjoy the pleasure of a divine voice, which, though it be often beard, I long to hear again; not that I am overcome with the charm of a voluptuous voice, but I am being taught divine mysteries, and expect as the result, not death but eternal salvation. For the singers are not the deadly Sirens of the Greeks, but a divine choir of prophets, with whom there is no need to stop the ears of one's companions, nor to load one's-self with bonds, in fear of the penalty of hearing. For, in the one case, the hearer, with the entrance of the voice, ceases to live; in the other, the more he hears, the better life will he enjoy, being led onwards by a divine Spirit. Let everyone come, then, and hear the divine song without any fear. There are not with us the Sirens from the shore of Sicily, nor the bonds of Ulysses, nor the wax poured melting into men's ears; but a loosening of all bonds, and liberty to listen to everyone that approaches. For it is worthy of us to hear such a song as this; and to hear such singers as these, seems to me to be a thing to be prayed for. But if one wishes to hear the choir of the apostles as well, he will find the same harmony of song. For the others sang beforehand the divine plan in a mystical manner; but these sing an interpretation of what has been mystically announced by the former. Oh, concordant harmony, composed by the Divine Spirit! Oh, the comeliness of those who sing of the mysteries *of God!* Oh, that I also may join in these songs in my prayer. Let us then also sing the like song, and raise the hymn to the Holy Father, glorifying in the Spirit Jesus, who is in His bosom.

Shun not, man, a spiritual hymn, nor be ill-disposed to listen to it. Death belongs not to it; a story of salvation is our song. Already I seem to taste better enjoyments, as I discourse on such subjects as these; and especially when there is before me such a flowering meadow, that is to say, our assembly of those who unite in singing and hearing the divine mysteries. Wherefore I dare to ask you to listen to me with ears free from all envy, without imitating the jealousy of Cain, or persecuting your brother, like Esau, or approving the brethren of Joseph, because they hated their brother on account of his words; but differing far from all these, insomuch that each of you is used to speak the mind of his neighbor. And, on this account, there is no evil jealousy among you, as ye have undertaken to supply your brother's deficiencies. O noble audience, and venerable company, and spiritual food! That I may ever have a right to share in such pleasures, be this my prayer!

Valentinian. As I was walking yesterday evening, my friend, along the shore of the sea, and was gazing on it somewhat intently, I saw an extraordinary instance of divine power, and a work of art produced by wise science, if at least such a thing may be called a work of art. For as that verse of Homer says,—

"As when two adverse winds blowing from Thrace,
Boreas and Zephyrus, the fishy deep
Vex sudden, all around, the sable flood
High curled, flings forth the salt weed on the shore;"—

So it seemed to me to have happened yesterday. For I saw waves very like mountaintops, and, so to speak, reaching up to heaven itself. Whence I expected nothing else but that the whole land would be deluged, and I began to form in my mind a place of escape, and a Noah's ark. But it was not as I thought; for, just as the sea rose to a crest, it broke up again into itself, without overstepping its own limits, having, so to speak, a feeling of awe for a divine decree. And as oftentimes a servant, compelled by his master to do something against his will, obeys the command through fear, while he dares not say a word of what he suffers in his unwillingness to do it, but, full of rage, mutters to himself,—somewhat so it appeared to me that the sea, as if enraged and confining its awe within itself, kept itself under, as not willing to let its Master perceive its anger.

On these occurrences I began to gaze in silence, and wished to measure in my mind the heaven and its sphere. I began to inquire whence it rises and where it sets; also what sort of motion it had—whether a progressive one, that is to say, one from place to place, or a revolving one; and, besides, how its movement is continued. And, of a truth, it seemed worthwhile to inquire also about the sun,—what is the manner of his being set in the heaven; also what is the orbit he traverses; also whither it is that, after a short time, he retires; and why it is that even he does not go out of his proper course: but he, too, as one may say, is observing a commandment of a higher power, and appears with us just when he is allowed to do so, and departs as if he were called away.

So, as I was investigating these things, I saw that the sunshine was departing, and the daylight failing, and that immediately darkness came on; and the sun was succeeded by the moon, who, at her first rising, was not of full size, but after advancing in her course presented a larger appearance. And I did not cease inquiring about her also, but examined the cause of her waning and waxing, and why it is that she, too, observes the revolution of days; and it seemed to me from all this that there is a divine government and power controlling the whole, which we may justly call God.

And thereupon I began to praise the Creator, as I saw the earth fast fixed, and living creatures in such variety, and the blossoms of plants with their many hues. But my mind did not rest upon these things alone; but thereupon I began to inquire whence they have their origin—whether from some source eternally co-existent with God, or from Himself alone, none co-existing with

Him; for that He has made nothing out of that which has no existence appeared to me the right view to take, unless my reason were altogether untrustworthy. For it is the nature of things which come into being to derive their origin from what is already existing. And it seemed to me that it might be said with equal truth, that nothing is eternally co-existent with God distinct from Himself, but that whatever exists has its origin from Him, and I was persuaded of this also by the undeniable disposition of the elements, and by the orderly arrangement of nature about them.

So, with some such thoughts of the fair order of things, I returned home. But on the day following, that is today, as I came I saw two beings of the same race—I mean men—striking and abusing one another; and another, again, wishing to strip his neighbor. And now some began to venture upon a more terrible deed; for one stripped a corpse, and exposed again to the light of day a body that had been once hidden in the earth, and treated a form like his own with such insult as to leave the corpse to be food for dogs; while another bared his sword, and attacked a man like himself. And he wanted to procure safety by flight; but the other ceased not from pursuing, nor would control his anger. And why should I say more? It is enough that he attacked him, and at once smote him with his sword. So *the wounded man* became a suppliant to his fellow, and spread out his hands in supplication, and was willing to give up his clothing, and only made a claim for life. But the other did not subdue his anger, nor pity his fellowman, nor would he see his own image in the being before him; but, like a wild beast, made preparations with his sword for feeding upon him. And now he was even putting his mouth to the body so like his own, such was the extent of his rage. And there was to be seen one man suffering injurious treatment, and another forthwith stripping him, and not even covering with earth the body which he denuded of clothing. But, in addition to these, there was another who, robbing others of their marriage rights, wanted to insult his neighbor's wife, and urged her to turn to unlawful embraces, not wishing her husband to be father to a child of his own.

After that I began to believe the tragedies, and thought that the dinner of Thyestes had really taken place; and believed in the unlawful lust of Oinomaos, nor doubted of the strife in which brother drew the sword on brother.

So, after beholding such things as these, I began to inquire whence they arise, and what is their origin, and who is the author of such devices against men, whence came their discovery, and who is the teacher of them. Now to dare to say that God was the author of these things was impossible; for surely it could not even be said that they have from Him their substance, or their existence. For how were it possible to entertain these thoughts of God? For He is good, and the Creator of what is excellent, and to Him belongs nothing bad. Nay, it is His nature to take no pleasure in such things; but He forbids their production, and rejects those who delight in them, but admits into His presence those who avoid them. And how could it be anything but absurd to call God the maker of these things of which He disapproves? For He would not wish them not to be, if He had first been their creator; and He wishes those who approach Him to be imitators of Him.

Wherefore it seemed to me unreasonable to attribute these things to God, or to speak of them as having sprung from Him; though it must certainly be granted that it is possible for something to come into existence out of what has no existence, in case He made what is evil. For He who brought them into existence out of non-existence would not reduce them to the loss of it. And again, it must be said that there was once a time when God took pleasure in evil things, which now is not the case. Wherefore it seems to me impossible to say this of God. For it is unsuitable to His nature to attach this to Him. Wherefore it seemed to me that there is co-existent with Him somewhat which has the name of matter, from which He formed existing things, distinguishing between them with wise art, and arranging them in a fair order, from which also evil things seem to have come into being. For as this matter was without quality or form, and, besides this, was borne about without order, and was untouched by divine art, God bore no grudge against it, nor left it to be continually thus borne about, but began to work upon it, and wished to separate its best parts from its worst, and thus made all that it was fitting for God to make out of it; but so much of it as was like lees, so to speak, this being unfitted for being made into anything, He left as it was, since it was of no use to Him; and from this it seems to me that what is evil has now streamed down among men. This seemed to me the right view to take of these things. But, my friend, if you think that anything I have said is wrong, mention it, for I exceedingly desire to hear about these things.

Orthodoxus. I appreciate your readiness, my friend, and applaud your zeal about the subject; and as for the opinion which you have expressed respecting existing things, to the effect that God made them out of some underlying substance, I do not altogether find fault with it.

For, truly, the origin of evil *is a subject that* has called out opinions from many men. Before you and me, no doubt, there have been many able men who have made the most searching inquiry into the matter. And some of them expressed the same opinion as you did, but others again represented God as the creator of these things, fearing to allow the existence of substance as coeval with Him; while the former, from fear of saying that God was the author of evil, thought fit to represent matter as coeval with Him. And it was the fate of both of these to fail to speak rightly on the subject, in consequence of their fear of God not being in agreement with an accurate knowledge of the truth.

But others declined to inquire about such a question at all, on the ground that such an inquiry is endless. As for me, however, my connection with you in friendship does not allow me to decline the subject of inquiry, especially when you announce your own purpose, that you are not swayed by prejudice,—although you had your opinion about the condition of things derived from your conjectures,—but say that you are confirmed in a desire of knowing the truth.

Wherefore I will willingly turn to the discussion of the question. But I wish this companion of mine here to listen to our conversation. For, indeed, he seems to have much the same opinions about these things as you have, wherefore I wish that you should both have a share in the discussion. For whatever I should say to you, situated as you are, I shall say just as much to him. If, then, you are indulgent enough to think I speak truly on this great subject, give an answer to each question I ask; for the result of this will be that you will gain a knowledge of the truth, and I shall not carry on my discussion with you at random.

Valentinian. I am ready to do as you say; and therefore be quite ready to ask those questions from which you think I may be able to gain an accurate knowledge of this important subject. For the object which I have set before myself is not the base one of gaining a victory, but that of becoming thoroughly acquainted with the truth. Wherefore apply yourself to the rest of the discussion.

Orthodoxus. Well, then, I do not suppose you are ignorant that it is impossible for two uncreated things to exist together, although you seem to have expressed nearly as much as this in an earlier part of the conversation. Assuredly we must of necessity say one of two things: either that God is separate from matter, or, on the other hand, that He is inseparable from it. If, then, one would say that they are united, he will say that that which is uncreated is one only, for each of the things spoken of will be a part of the other; and as they are parts of each other, there will not be two uncreated things, but one composed of different elements. For we do not, because a man has different members, break him up into many beings. But, as the demands of reason require, we say that a single being, man, of many parts, has been created by God. So it is necessary, if God be not separate from matter, to say that that which is uncreated is one only; but if one shall say that He is separate, there must necessarily be something intermediate between the two, which makes their separation evident. For it is impossible to estimate the distance of one thing from another, unless there be something else with which the distance between them may be compared. And this holds good, not only as far as the instance before us, but also to any number of others. For the argument which we advanced in the case of two uncreated things would of necessity be of equal force, were the uncreated things granted to be three in number. For I should ask also respecting them, whether they are separate from each other, or, on the other hand, are united each to its neighbor. For if anyone resolve to say that they are united, he will be told the same as before; if, again, that they are separate, he will not escape the necessary existence of that which separates them.

If, then, any one were to say that there is a third account which might fitly be given of uncreated things, namely, that neither is God separate from matter, nor, again, are they united as part of a whole; but that God is locally situate in matter, and matter in God, he must be told as the consequence, that if we say that God is placed in matter, we must of necessity say that He is contained within limits, and circumscribed by matter. But then He must, equally with matter, be carried about without order. And that He rests not, nor remains by Himself, is a necessary result of that in which He is being carried, now this way, and now that. And besides this, we must say that God was in worse case still.

For if matter were once without order, and He, determining to change it for the better, put it into order, there was a time when God was in that which had no order. And I might fairly ask this question also, whether God filled matter completely, or existed in some part of it. For if one resolve to say that God was in some part of matter, how far smaller than matter does he make Him; that is, if a part of it contained God altogether. But if he were to say that He is in all of it, and is extended through the whole of matter, he must tell us how He wrought upon it. For we must say that there was a sort of contraction of God, which being effected, He wrought upon that from which He was withdrawn, or else that He wrought in union with matter, without having a place of withdrawal. But if anyone say that matter is in God, there is equal need of inquiry, namely, whether it is by His being separated from Himself, and as creatures exist in the air, by His being divided and parted for the reception of the beings that are in Him; or whether it is locally situated, that is to say, as water in land; for if we were to say, as in the air, we must say that God is divisible; but if, as water in earth,—since matter was without order and arrangement, and besides, contained what was evil,—we must say, that in God were to be found the disorderly and the evil. Now this seems to me an unbecoming conclusion, nay, more a dangerous one. For you wish for the existence of matter, that you may avoid saying that God is the author of evil; and, determining to avoid this, you say that He is the receptacle of evil.

If, then, under the supposition that matter is separate from created substances, you had said that it is uncreated, I should have said much about it, to prove that it is impossible for it to be uncreated; but since you say that the *question of* the origin of evil is the cause of this supposition, it therefore seems to me right to proceed to inquire into this. For when it is clearly stated how evil exists, and that it is not possible to say that God is the cause of evil, because of matter being subject to Him, it seems to me to destroy such a supposition, to remark, that if God created the qualities which did not exist, He equally created the substances.

Do you say then, that there co-exists with God matter without qualities out of which He formed the beginning of this world?

Valentinian. So I think.

Orthodoxus. If, then, matter had no qualities, and the world were produced by God, and qualities exist in the world, then God is the maker of qualities?

Valentinian. It is so.

Orthodoxus. Now, as I heard you say some time ago that it is impossible for anything to come into being out of that which has no existence, answer my question: Do you think that the qualities of the world were not produced out of any existing qualities?

Valentinian. I do.

Orthodoxus. And that they are something distinct from substances?

Valentinian. Yes.

Orthodoxus. If, then, qualities were neither made by God out of any ready at hand, nor derive their existence from substances, because they are not substances, we must say that they were produced by God out of what had no existence. Wherefore I thought you spoke extravagantly in saying that it was impossible to suppose that anything was produced by God out of what did not exist.

But let our discussion of this matter stand thus. For truly we see among ourselves men making things out of what does not exist, although they seem for the most part to be making them with something. As, for instance, we may have an example in the case of architects; for they truly do not make cities out of cities, nor in like manner temples out of temples.

But if, because substances underlie these things, you think that the builders make them out of what does exist, you are mistaken in your calculation. For it is not the substance which makes the city or the temples, but art applied to substance. And this art is not produced out of some art which lies in the substances themselves, but from that which is not in them.

But you seem likely to meet me with this argument: that the artificer makes the art which is connected with the substance out of the art which he has. Now I think it is a good reply to this to say, that in man it is not produced from any art lying beneath; for it is not to be granted that substance by itself is art. For art is in the class of accidents, and is one of the things that have an existence only when they are employed about some substance. For man will exist even without the art of building, but it will have no existence unless man be previously in being. Whence we must say that it is in the nature of things for arts to be produced in men out of what has no existence. If, then, we have shown that this is so in the case of men, why was it improper to say that God is able to make not only qualities, but also substances, out of that which has no existence? For as it appears possible for something to be produced out of what exists not, it is evident that this is the case with substances. To return to the question of evil. Do you think evil comes under the head of substances, or of qualities of substances?

Valentinian. Of qualities.

Orthodoxus. But matter was found to be without quality or form?

Valentinian. It was.

Orthodoxus. Well, then, the connection of these names with substance is owing to its accidents. For murder is not a substance, nor is any other evil; but the substance receives a cognate name from putting it into practice. For a man is not (spoken of as) murder, but by committing it he receives the derived name of murderer, without being himself murder; and, to speak concisely, no other evil is a substance; but by practicing any evil, it can be called evil. Similarly consider, if you imagine anything else to be the cause of evil to men, that it too is evil by reason of its acting by them, and suggesting the committal of evil. For a man is evil in consequence of his actions. For he is said to be evil, because he is the doer of evil. Now what a man does, is not the man himself, but his activity, and it is from his actions that he receives the title of evil. For if we were to say that he is that which he does, and he commits murders, adulteries, and such-like, he will be all these. Now if he is these, then when they are produced he has an existence, but when they are not, he too ceases to be. Now these things are produced by men. Men then will be the authors of them, and the causes of their existing or not existing. But if each man is evil in consequence of what he practices, and what he practices has an origin, he also made a beginning in evil, and evil too had a beginning. Now if this is the case, no one is without a beginning in evil, nor are evil things without an origin.

 Valentinian. Well, my friend, you seem to me to have argued sufficiently against the other side. For you appeared to draw right conclusions from the premises which we granted to the discussion. For truly if matter is without qualities, then God is the maker of qualities; and if evils are qualities, God will be the author of evils. But it seems to me false to say that matter is without qualities; for it cannot be said respecting any substance that it is without qualities. But indeed, in the very act of saying that it is without qualities, you declare that it has a quality, by describing the character of matter, which is a kind of quality. Therefore, if you please, begin the discussion from the beginning; for it seems to me that matter never began to have qualities. For such being the case, I assert, my friend, that evil arises from its emanation.

Orthodoxus. If matter were possessed of qualities from eternity, of what will God be the creator? For if we say substances, we speak of them as pre-existing; if, again, we say qualities, these too are declared to have an existence. Since, then, both substances and qualities exist, it seems to me superfluous to call God a creator. But answer me a question. In what way do you say that God was a creator? Was it by changing the existence of those substances into non-existence, or by changing the qualities while He preserved the substances?

Valentinian. I think that there was no change of the substances, but only of the qualities; and in respect to these we call God a creator. And just as if one might chance to say that a house was made of stones, it cannot be said of them that they do not still continue stones in substance, because they are called a house; for I affirm that the house is made by the quality of construction. So I think that God, while substance remained, produced a change of its qualities, by reason of which I say that this world was made by God.

Orthodoxus. Do you think, too, that evil is among the qualities of substances?

Valentinian. I do.

Orthodoxus. And were these qualities in matter from the first, or had they a beginning?

Valentinian. I say that these qualities were eternally co-existent with matter.

Orthodoxus. But do you not say that God has made a change in the qualities?

Valentinian. I do say this.

Orthodoxus. For the better?

Valentinian. I think so.

Orthodoxus. If, then, evil is among the qualities of matter, and its qualities were changed by God for the better, the inquiry must be made whence evil arose. For either all of them, being evil, underwent a change for the better, or some of them being evil, and some not, the evil ones were not changed for the better; but the rest, as far as they were found superior, were changed by God for the sake of order.

Valentinian. That is the opinion I held from the beginning.

Orthodoxus. How, then, do you say it was that He left the qualities of evil as they were? Was it that He was able to do away with them, or that, though He wished to do so, He was unable? For if you say that He was able, but disinclined to do so, He must be the author of these things; because, while He had power to bring evil to an end, He allowed it to remain as it was, especially when He had begun to work upon matter. For if He had had nothing at all to do with matter, He would not have been the author of what He allowed to remain. But since He works upon a part of it, and leaves a part of it to itself, while He has power to change it for the better, I think He is the author of evil, since He left part of matter in its vileness. He wrought then for the ruin of a part; and, in this respect, it seems to me that this part was chiefly injured by His arranging it in matter, so that it became partaker of evil. For before matter was put in order, it was without the perception of evil; but now each of its parts has the capacity of perceiving evil. Now, take an example in the case of man. Previously to becoming a living creature, he was insensible to evil; but from the time when he is fashioned by God into the form of man, he gains the perception of approaching evil. So this act of God, which you say was done for the benefit of matter, is found to have happened to it rather for the worse. But if you say that God was not able to stop evil, does the impossibility result from His being naturally weak, or from His being overcome by fear, and in subjection to some more powerful being? See which of these you would like to attribute to the almighty and good God. But, again, answer me about matter. Is matter simple or compound? For if matter be simple and uniform, and the universe compound, and composed of different substances, it is impossible to say that it is made of matter, because compound things cannot be composed of one pure and simple ingredient. For composition indicates the mixture of several simple things. But if, on the other hand, you say that matter is compound, it has been entirely composed of simple elements, and they were once each separately simple, and by their composition matter was produced; for compound things derive their composition from simple things. So there was once a time when matter did not exist—that is to say, before the combination of the simple elements. But if there was once a time when matter did not exist, and there was never a time when what is uncreated did not exist, then matter is not uncreated. And from this it follows that there are many things which are uncreated. For if God were uncreated, and the simple elements of which matter was composed were uncreated, the number of the uncreated would be more than two. But to omit inquiring what are the simple elements, matter or form—for this would be followed by many absurdities—let me ask, do you think that nothing that exists is contrary to itself?

Valentinian. I do.

Orthodoxus. Yet water is contrary to fire, and darkness to light, and heat to cold, and moisture to dryness.

Valentinian. I think it is.

Orthodoxus. If, then, nothing that exists is contrary to itself, and these are contrary to one another, they will not be one and the same matter—no, nor formed from one and the same matter. But, again, I wish to ask, do you think that the parts of a thing are not destructive of one another?

Valentinian. I do.

Orthodoxus. And that fire and water, and the rest likewise, are parts of matter?

Valentinian. I hold them to be so.

Orthodoxus. Why, then, do you not think that water is destructive of fire, and light of darkness, and so on with the rest?

Valentinian. I do.

Orthodoxus. Then, if parts of a thing are not destructive of one another, and these are found to be so, they will not be parts of the same thing. But if they are not parts of the same thing, they will not be parts of one and the same matter. And, indeed, they will not be matter either, because nothing that exists is destructive of itself. And this being the case with the contraries, it is shown that they are not matter. This is enough on the subject of matter.

Now we must come to the examination of evils, and must necessarily inquire into the evils among men. As to these, are they forms of the principle of evil, or parts of it? If forms, evil will not have a separate existence distinct from them, because the species are to be sought for in the forms, and underlie them. But if this is the case, evil has an origin. For its forms are shown to have an origin—such as murder, and adultery, and the like. But if you will have them to be parts of some principle of evil, and they have an origin, it also must have an origin. For those things whose parts have an origin, are of necessity originated likewise. For the whole consists of parts. And the whole will not exist if the parts do not, though there may be some parts, even if the whole be not there.

Now there is nothing existing of which one part is originated, and another part not. But if I were even to grant this, then there was a time when evil was not complete, namely, before matter was wrought by God. And it attains completeness when man is produced by God; for man is the maker of the parts of evil. And from this it follows that the cause of evil being complete, is God the Creator, which it is impious to say. But if you say that evil is neither of the things supposed, but is the doing of something evil, you declare that it has an origin. For the doing of a thing makes the beginning of its existence. And besides this, you have nothing further to pronounce evil. For what other action have you to point out as such, except what happens among men? Now, it has been already shown that he who acts is not evil according to his being, but in accordance with his evil doing.

Because there is nothing evil by nature, but it is by use that evil things become such. So I say, says he, that man was made with a free-will, not as if there were already evil in existence, which he had the power of choosing if he wished, but on account of his capacity of obeying or disobeying God.

For this was the meaning of the gift of Free Will. And man after his creation receives a commandment from God; and from this at once rises evil, for he does not obey the divine command; and this alone is evil, namely, disobedience, which had a beginning.

• • • • • •

For man received power, and enslaved himself, not because he was overpowered by the irresistible tendencies of his nature, nor because the capacity with which he was gifted deprived him of what was better for him; for it was for the sake of this that I say he was endowed with it (but he received the power above mentioned), in order that he may obtain an addition to what he already possesses, which accrues to him from the Superior Being in consequence of his obedience, and is demanded as a debt from his Maker. For I say that man was made not for destruction, but for better things. For if he were made as any of the elements, or those things which render a similar service to God, he would cease to receive a reward befitting deliberate choice, and would be like an instrument of the maker; and it would be unreasonable for him to suffer blame for his wrong-doings, for the real author of them is the one by whom he is used. But man did not understand better things, since he did not know the author (of his existence), but only the object for which he was made. I say therefore that God, purposing thus to honor man, and to grant him an understanding of better things, has given him the power of being able to do what he wishes, and commends the employment of his power for better things; not that He deprives him again of free-will, but wishes to point out the better way. For the power is present with him, and he receives the commandment; but God exhorts him to turn his power of choice to better things. For as a father exhorts his son, who has power to learn his lessons, to give more attention to them inasmuch as, while he points out this as the better course, he does not deprive his son of the power which he possessed, even if he be not inclined to learn willingly; so I do not think that God, while He urges on man to obey His commands, deprives him of the power of purposing and withholding obedience. For He points out the cause of His giving this advice, in that He does not deprive him of the power. But He gives commands, in order that man may be able to enjoy better things. For this is the consequence of obeying the commands of God. So that He does not give commands in order to take away the power which He has given, but in order that a better gift may be bestowed, as to one worthy of attaining greater things, in return for his having rendered obedience to God, while he had power to withhold it. I say that man was made with free-will, not as if there were already existing some evil, which he had the power of choosing if he wished,...but that the power of obeying and disobeying God is the only cause.

For this was the object to be obtained by free-will. And man after his creation receives a commandment from God, and from this at once rises evil; for he does not obey the divine command, and this alone is evil, namely, disobedience, which had a beginning. For no one has it in his power to say that it is without an origin, when its author had an origin. But you will be sure to ask whence arose this disobedience. It is clearly recorded in Holy Scripture, by which I am enabled to say that man was not made by God in this condition, but that he has come to it by some teaching. For man did not receive such a nature as this. For if it were the case that his nature was such, this would not have come upon him by teaching. Now one says in Holy Writ, that "man has learnt (evil)." I say, then, that disobedience to God is taught. For this alone is evil which is produced in opposition to the purpose of God, for man would not learn evil by itself. He, then, who teaches evil is the Serpent.

・・・・・・

For my part, I said that the beginning of evil was envy, and that it arose from man's being distinguished by God with higher honor. Now evil is disobedience to the commandment of God.

From the Discourse on the Resurrection.
───────────────

Part I.
I. God did not make evil, nor is He at all in any way the author of evil; but whatever failed to keep the law, which He in all justice ordained, after being made by Him with the faculty of free-will, for the purpose of guarding and keeping it, is called evil. Now it is the gravest fault to disobey God, by overstepping the bounds of that righteousness which is consistent with free-will.

II. Now the question has already been raised, and answered, that the "coats of skins" are not bodies.

Nevertheless, let us speak of it again, for it is not enough to have mentioned it once. Before the preparation of these coats of skins, the first man himself acknowledges that he has both bones and flesh; for when he saw the woman brought to him: "This is now," he cried, "bone of my bone and flesh of my flesh." And again: She shall be called Woman, because she was taken out of man. For this cause shall a man leave his father and mother, and shall be joined unto his wife, and they two shall be one flesh." For I cannot endure the trifling of some who shamelessly do violence to Scripture, in order that their opinion, that the resurrection is without flesh, may find support; supposing rational bones and flesh, and in different ways changing it backwards and forwards by allegorizing. And Christ confirms the taking of these things as they are written, when, to the question of the Pharisees about putting away a wife, He answers: "Have ye not read that He which made them at the beginning made them male and female; and said, For this cause shall a man leave his father," and so on.

III. But it is evidently absurd to think that the body will not co-exist with the soul in the eternal state, because it is a bond and fetters; in order that, according to their view, we who are to live in the kingdom of light may not be forever condemned to be bondmen of corruption. For as the question has been sufficiently solved, and the statement refitted in which they defined the flesh to be the soul's chain, the argument also is destroyed, that the flesh will not rise again, lest, if we resume it, we be prisoners in the kingdom of light.

IV. In order, then, that man might not be an undying or ever-living evil, as would have been the case if sin were dominant within him, as it had sprung up in an immortal body, and was provided with immortal sustenance, God for this cause pronounced him mortal, and clothed him with mortality. For this is what was meant by the coats of skins, in order that, by the dissolution of the body, sin might be altogether destroyed from the very roots, that there might not be left even the smallest particle of root from which new shoots of sin might again burst forth.

V. For as a fig-tree, which has grown in the splendid buildings of a temple, and has reached a great size, and is spread over all the joints of the stones with thickly-branching roots, ceases not to grow, till, by the loosening of the stones from the place in which it sprung up, it is altogether torn away; for it is possible for the stones to be fitted into their own places, when the fig tree is taken away, so that the temple may be preserved, having no longer to support what was the cause of its own destruction; while the fig-tree, torn away by the roots, dies; in the same way also, God, the builder, checked by the seasonable application of death, His own temple, man, when he had fostered sin, like a wild fig-tree, "killing," in the words of Scripture, "and making alive," in order that the flesh, after sin is withered and dead, may, like a restored temple, be raised up again with the same parts, uninjured and immortal, while sin is utterly and entirely destroyed. For while the body still lives, before it has passed through death, sin must also live with it, as it has its roots concealed within us even though it be externally checked by the wounds inflicted by corrections and warnings; since, otherwise, it would not happen that we do wrong after baptism, as we should be entirely and absolutely free from sin. But now, even after believing, and after the time of being touched by the water of sanctification, we are oftentimes found in sin. For no one can boast of being so free from sin as not even to have an evil thought. So that it is come to pass that sin is now restrained and lulled to sleep by faith, so that it does not produce injurious fruits, but yet is not torn up by the roots. For the present we restrain its sprouts, such as evil imaginations, "lest any root of bitterness springing up trouble" us, not suffering its leaves to unclose and open into shoots; while the Word, like an axe, cuts at its roots which grow below. But hereafter the very thought of evil will disappear.

VI. But come now, since there is need of many examples in matters of this kind, let us examine them particularly from this point of view, without desisting till our argument ends in clearer explanation and proof. It appears, then, as if an eminent craftsman were to cast over again a noble image, wrought by himself of gold or other material, and beautifully proportioned in all its members, upon his suddenly perceiving that it had been mutilated by some infamous man, who, too envious to endure the image being beautiful, spoiled it, and thus enjoyed the empty pleasure of indulged jealousy. For take notice, most wise Aglaophon, that, if the artificer wish that that upon which he has bestowed so much pains and care and labor, shall be quite free from injury, he will be impelled to melt it down, and restore it to its former condition. But if he should not cast it afresh, nor reconstruct it, but allow it to remain as it is, repairing and restoring it, it must be that the image, being passed through the fire and forged, cannot any longer be preserved unchanged, but will be altered and wasted. Wherefore, if he should wish it to be perfectly beautiful and faultless, it must be broken up and recast, in order that all the disfigurements and mutilations inflicted upon it by treachery and envy, may be got rid of by the breaking up and recasting of it, while the image is restored again uninjured and unalloyed to the same form as before, and made as like itself as possible. For it is impossible for an image under the hands of the original artist to be lost, even if it be melted down again, for it may be restored; but it is possible for blemishes and injuries to be put off, for they melt away and cannot be restored; because in every work of art the best craftsman looks not for blemish or failure, but for symmetry and correctness in his work. Now God's plan seems to me to have been the same as that which prevails among ourselves. For seeing man, His fairest work, corrupted by envious treachery, He could not endure, with His love for man, to leave him in such a condition, lest he should be forever faulty, and bear the blame to eternity; but dissolved him again into his original materials, in order that, by remodeling, all the blemishes in him might waste away and disappear. For the melting down of the statue in the former case corresponds to the death and dissolution of the body in the latter, and the remolding of the material in the former, to the resurrection after death in the latter; as also says the prophet Jeremiah, for he addresses *the Jews* in these words, "And I went down to the potter's house; and, behold, he wrought a work upon the stones. And the vessel which he made in his hands was broken; and again he made another vessel, as it pleased him to make it. And the word of the Lord came to me, saying, Cannot I do to you as this potter, O house of Israel? Behold, as the clay of the potter are ye in my hands."

VII. For I call your attention to this, that, as I said, after man's transgression the Great Hand was not content to leave as a trophy of victory its own work, debased by the Evil One, who wickedly injured it from motives of envy; but moistened and reduced it to clay, as a potter breaks up a vessel, that by the remodeling of it all the blemishes and bruises in it may disappear, and it may be made afresh faultless and pleasing.

VIII. But it is not satisfactory to say that the universe will be utterly destroyed, and sea and air and sky will be no longer. For the whole world will be deluged with fire from heaven, and burnt for the purpose of purification and renewal; it will not, however, come to complete ruin and corruption. For if it were better for the world not to be than to be, why did God, in making the world, take the worse course? But God did not work in vain, or do that which was worst. God therefore ordered the creation with a view to its existence and continuance, as also the *Book of Wisdom* confirms, saying, "For God created all things that they might have their being; and the generations of the world were healthful, and there is no poison of destruction in them." And Paul clearly testifies this, saying, "For the earnest expectation of the creature waited for the manifestation of the sons of God. For the creature was made subject to vanity, not willingly, but by reason of him that subjected the same in hope: because the creature itself also shall be delivered from the bondage of corruption into the glorious liberty of the children of God." For the creation was made subject to vanity, he says, and he expects that it will be set free from such servitude, as he intends to call this world by the name of creation. For it is not what is unseen but what is seen that is subject to corruption. The creation, then, after being restored to a better and more seemly state, remains, rejoicing and exulting over the children of God at the resurrection; for whose sake it now groans and travails, waiting itself also for our redemption from the corruption of the body, that, when we have risen and shaken off the mortality of the flesh, according to that which is written, "Shake off the dust, and arise, and sit down, O Jerusalem," and have been set free from sin, it also shall be freed from corruption and be subject no longer to vanity, but to righteousness. Isaiah says, too, "For as the new heaven and the new earth which I make, remained before me, says the Lord, so shall your seed and your name be;" and again, "Thus says the Lord that created the heaven, it is He who prepared the earth and created it, He determined it; He created it not in vain, but formed it to be inhabited." For in reality God did not establish the universe in vain, or to no purpose but destruction, as those weak-minded men say, but to exist, and be inhabited, and continue. Wherefore the earth and the heaven must exist again after the conflagration and shaking of all things.

IX. But if our opponents say, How then is it, if the universe be not destroyed, that the Lord says that "heaven and earth shall pass away;" and the prophet, that "the heaven shall perish as smoke, and the earth shall grow old as a garment;" we answer, because it is usual for the Scriptures to call the change of the world from its present condition to a better and more glorious one, destruction; as its earlier form is lost in the change of all things to a state of greater splendor; for there is no contradiction nor absurdity in the Holy Scriptures. For not "the world" but the "fashion of this world" passes away, it is said; so it is usual for the Scriptures to call the change from an earlier form to a better and more comely state, destruction; just as when one calls by the name of destruction the change from a childish form into a perfect man, as the stature of the child is turned into *manly* size and beauty. We may expect that the creation will pass away, as if it were to perish in the burning, in order that it may be renewed, not however that it will be destroyed, that we who are renewed may dwell in a renewed world without taste of sorrow; according as it is said, "When Thou lets Thy breath go forth, they shall be made, and Thou shalt renew the face of the earth;" God henceforth providing for the due temperature of that which surrounds it. For as the earth is to exist after the present age, there must be by all means inhabitants for it, who shall no longer be liable to death, nor shall marry, nor beget children, but live in all happiness, like the angels, without change or decay. Wherefore it is silly to discuss in what way of life our bodies will then exist, if there is no longer air, nor earth, nor anything else.

X. But in addition to what has been said, there is this point worth consideration, since it misleads very much, if we may be outspoken about matters of such importance, Aglaophon. For you said that the Lord declared plainly that those who shall obtain the resurrection shall then be as the angels. You brought this objection: The angels, being without flesh, are on this account in the utmost happiness and glory. We must then, as we are to be made equal to the angels, be like them stripped of flesh, and be angels. But you overlooked this, my excellent friend, that He who created and set in order the universe out of nothing, ordained the nature of immortal beings to be distributed not only among angels and ministers, but also among principalities, and thrones, and powers. For the race of angels is one, and that of principalities and powers another; because immortal beings are not all of one order, and constitution, and tribe, and family, but there are differences of race and tribe. And neither do the cherubim, departing from their own nature, assume the form of angels; nor, again, do angels assume the form of the others. For they cannot be anything but what they are and have been made. Moreover, man also having been appointed by the original order of things to inhabit the world, and to rule over all that is in it, when he is immortal, will never be changed from being a man into the form either of angels or any other; for neither do angels undergo a change from their original form to another. For Christ at His coming did not proclaim that the human nature should, when it is immortal, be remolded or transformed into another nature, but into what it was before the fall. For each one among created things must remain in its own proper place, that none may be wanting to any, but all may be full: heaven of angels, thrones of powers, luminaries of ministers; and the more divine spots, and the undefiled and untainted luminaries, with seraphim, who attend the Supreme Council, and uphold the universe; and the world of men. For if we granted that men are changed into angels, it would follow that we say that angels also are changed into powers, and these into one thing and the other, until our argument proceed too far for safety.

XI. Neither did God, as if He had made man badly, or committed a mistake in the formation of him, determine afterwards to make an angel, repenting of His work, as the worst of craftsmen do; nor did He fashion man, after He had wished originally to make an angel, and failed; for this would be a sign of weakness, etc. Why even then did He make man and not angels, if He wished men to be angels and not men? Was it because He was unable? It is blasphemy to suppose so. Or was He so busy in making the worse as to loiter about the better? This too is absurd. For He does not fail in making what is good, nor defers it, nor is incapable of it; but He has the power to act how and when He pleases, inasmuch as He is Himself power. Wherefore it was because He intended man to be man, that He originally made him so. But if He so intended—since He intends what is good—man is good. Now man is said to be composed of soul and body; he cannot then exist without a body, but with a body, unless there be produced another man besides man. For all the orders of immortal beings must be preserved by God, and among these is man. "For," says *the Book of Wisdom*, "God created man to be immortal, and made him to be an image of His own eternity." The body then perishes not; for man is composed of soul and body.

XII. Wherefore observe that these are the very things which the Lord wished to teach to the Sadducees, who did not believe in the resurrection of the flesh. For this was the opinion of the Sadducees. Whence it was that, having contrived the parable about the woman and the seven brethren, that they might cast doubt upon the resurrection of the flesh, "There came to Him," it is said, "the Sadducees also, who say that there is no resurrection." Christ, then, if there had been no resurrection of the flesh, but the soul only were saved, would have agreed with their opinion as a right and excellent one. But as it was, He answered and said, "In the resurrection they neither marry, nor are given in marriage, but are as the angels in heaven," not on account of having no flesh, but of not marrying nor being married, but being henceforth incorruptible. And He speaks of our being near the angels in this respect, that as the angels in heaven, so we also in paradise, spend our time no more in marriage-feasts or other festivities. But in seeing God and cultivating life, under the direction of Christ. For He did not say "they shall be angels," but like angels, in being, for instance, crowned, as it is written, with glory and honor; differing a little from the angels, while near to being angels. Just as if He had said, while observing the fair order of the sky, and the stillness of the night, and everything illumined by the heavenly light of the moon, "the moon shines like the sun." We should not then say that He asserted that the moon was absolutely the sun, but like the sun. As also that which is not gold, but approaching the nature of gold, is said not to be gold, but to be like gold. But if it were gold, it would be said to be, and not to be like, gold. But since it is not gold, but approaching to the nature of it, and has the appearance of it, it is said to be like gold; so also when He says that the saints shall. In the resurrection be like the angels, we do not understand Him to assert that they will then be actually angels, but approaching to the condition of angels. So that it is most unreasonable to say, "Since Christ declared that the saints in the resurrection appear as angels, therefore their bodies do not rise," although the very words employed give a clear proof of the real state of the case. For the term "resurrection" is not applied to that which has not fallen, but to that which has fallen and rises again; as when the prophet says, "I will also raise up again the tabernacle of David which has fallen down." Now the much-desired tabernacle of the soul is fallen, and sunk down into "the dust of the earth." For it is not that which is not dead, but that which is dead, that is laid down. But it is the flesh which dies; the soul is immortal. So, then, if the soul be immortal, and the body be the corpse, those who say that there is a resurrection, but not of the flesh, deny any resurrection; because it is not that which remains standing, but that which has fallen and been laid down, that is set up; according to that which is written, "Does not he who falls rise again, and he who turns aside return?"

XIII. Since flesh was made to border on incorruption and corruption, being itself neither the one nor the other, and was overcome by corruption for the sake of pleasure, though it was the work and property of incorruption; therefore it became corruptible, and was laid in the dust of the earth. When, then, it was overcome by corruption, and delivered over to death through disobedience, God did not leave it to corruption to be triumphed over as an inheritance; but, after conquering death by the resurrection, delivered it again to incorruption, in order that corruption might not receive the property of incorruption, but incorruption that of corruption. Therefore the apostle answers thus, "For this corruptible must put on incorruption, and this mortal must put on immortality." Now the corruptible and mortal putting on immortality, what else is it but that which is "sown in corruption and raised in incorruption,"—for the soul is not corruptible or mortal; but this which is mortal and corrupting is of flesh,—in order that, "as we have borne the image of the earthy, we shall also bear the image of the heavenly?" For the image of the earthy which we have borne is this, "Dust thou art, and unto dust shalt thou return." But the image of the heavenly is the resurrection from the dead, and incorruption, in order that "as Christ was raised up from the dead by the glory of the Father, so we also should walk in newness of life." But if any one were to think that the earthy image is the flesh itself, but the heavenly image some other spiritual body besides the flesh; let him first consider that Christ, the heavenly man, when He appeared, bore the same form of limbs and the same image of flesh as ours, through which also He, who was not man, became man, that "as in Adam all die, even so in Christ shall all be made alive." For if He bore flesh for any other reason than that of setting the flesh free, and raising it up, why did He bear flesh superfluously, as He purposed neither to save it, nor to raise it up? But the Son of God does nothing superfluously. He did not then take the form of a servant uselessly, but to raise it up and save it. For He truly was made man, and died, and not in mere appearance, but that He might truly be shown to be the first begotten from the dead, changing the earthy into the heavenly, and the mortal into the immortal. When, then, Paul says that "flesh and blood cannot inherit the kingdom of God," he does not give a disparaging opinion of the regeneration of the flesh, but would teach that the kingdom of God, which is eternal life, is not possessed by the body, but the body by the life. For if the kingdom of God, which is life, were possessed by the body, it would happen that the life would be consumed by corruption. But now the life possesses what is dying, in order that "death may be swallowed up in victory" by life, and the corruptible may be seen to be the possession of incorruption and immortality, while it becomes unbound and free from death and sin, but the slave and servant of immortality; so that the body may be the possession of incorruption, and not incorruption that of the body.

XIV. If, then, out of such a drop, small, and previously without any existence, in its actual state of moistness, contractedness, and insignificance, in fact out of nothing, man is brought into being, how much rather shall man spring again into being out of a previously existing man? For it is not so difficult to make anything anew after it has once existed and fallen into decay, as to produce out of nothing that which has never existed. Now, in case we choose to exhibit the seminal fluid discharged from a man, and place by it a corpse, each by itself, which of them, as they both lie exposed to view, will the spectators think most likely to become a man—that drop, which is nothing at all, or that which has already shape, and size, and substance? For if the very thing which is nothing at all, merely because God pleases, becomes a man, how much rather shall that which has existence and is brought to perfection become again a man, if God pleases? For what was the purpose of the theologian Moses, in introducing, under a mystical sense, the Feast of Tabernacles in the Book of Leviticus? Was it that we may keep a feast to God, as the Jews with their low view of the Scriptures interpret it? As if God took pleasure in such tabernacles, decked out with fruits and boughs and leaves, which immediately wither and lose their verdure. We cannot say so. Tell me, then, what was the object of the Feast of Tabernacles? It was introduced to point to this real tabernacle of ours, which, after it was fallen down to corruption through the transgression of the law, and broken up by sin, God promised to put together again, and to raise up in incorruptibility, in order that we may truly celebrate in His honor the great and renowned Feast of Tabernacles at the resurrection; when our tabernacles are put together in the perfect order of immortality and harmony, and raised up from the dust in incorruption; when the dry bones, according to the most true prophecy, shall hear a voice, and be brought to their joints by God, the Creator and Perfect Artificer, who will then renew the flesh and bind it on, no more with such ties as those by which it was at first held together, but by such as shall be forever undecaying and indissoluble. For I once saw on Olympus, which is a mountain of Lycia, fire bursting up from the ground spontaneously on the summit of the mountain; and by it was standing an Agnos tree, so flourishing, green, and shady, that one might suppose a never-failing stream of water had nourished its growth, rather than what was really the case. For which cause, therefore, though the natures of things are corruptible, and their bodies consumed by fire, and it is impossible for things which are once of an inflammable nature to remain unaffected by fire; yet this tree, so far from being burnt, is actually more vigorous and green than usual, though it is naturally inflammable, and that too when the fire is glowing about its very roots. I certainly cast some boughs of trees from the adjoining wood on to the place where the fire burst forth, and they immediately caught fire and were burnt to ashes. Now, then, tell me why it is that that which cannot bear even to feel the heat of the sun, but withers up under it unless it be sprinkled with water, is not consumed when beset by such fiery heat, but both lives and thrives? What is the meaning of this marvel? God appointed this as an example and introduction to the day that is coming, in order that we may know more certainly that, when all things are deluged with fire from heaven, the bodies which are distinguished by chastity and righteousness will be taken up by Him as free from all injury from the fire as from cold water. For truly, O beneficent and bountiful Lord, "the creature that serves Thee, who art the Maker, increases his strength against the unrighteous for their punishment, and abates his strength for the benefit of such as put their trust in Thee;" and at Thy pleasure fire cools, and injures nothing that Thou determines to be preserved; and again, water burns more fiercely than fire, and nothing opposes Thine unconquerable power and might. For Thou creates all things out of nothing; wherefore also Thou changes and transforms all things as Thou wilt, seeing they are Thine, and Thou alone art God.

XV. The apostle certainly, after assigning the planting and watering to art and earth and water, conceded the growth to God alone, where he says, "Neither is he that planted anything, neither he that watered; but God that giveth the increase." For he knew that Wisdom, the first-born of God, the parent and artificer of all things, brings forth everything into the world; whom the ancients called Nature and Providence, because she, with constant provision and care, gives to all things birth and growth. "For," says the Wisdom of God, "my Father worked hitherto, and I work." Now it is on this account that Solomon called Wisdom the artificer of all things, since God is in no respect poor, but able richly to create, and make, and vary, and increase all things.

XVI. God, who created all things, and provides and cares for all things, took dust from the ground, and made our outer man.

Part II.
The Second Discourse on the Resurrection.
For instance, then, the images of our kings here, even though they be not formed of the more precious materials—gold or silver—are honored by all. For men do not, while they treat with respect those of the far more precious material, slight those of a less valuable, but honor every image in the world, even though it be of

chalk or bronze. And one who speaks against either of them, is not acquitted as if he had only spoken against clay, nor condemned for having despised gold, but for having been disrespectful towards the King and Lord Himself. The images of God's angels, which are fashioned of gold, the principalities and powers, we make to His honor and glory.

Part III.

I. From the Discourse on the Resurrection.

I. Read the Book on the Resurrection by St. Methodius, Bishop and Martyr, of which that which follows is a selection, that the body is not the fetter of the soul, as Origen thought, nor are souls called by the prophet Jeremiah "fettered" on account of their being within bodies. For he lays down the principle that the body does not hinder the energies of the soul, but that rather the body is carried about with it, and cooperates in whatever the soul commits to it. But how are we to understand the opinion of Gregory the theologian, and many others?

II. That Origen said that the body was given to the soul as a fetter after the fall, and that previously it lived without a body; but that this body which we wear is the cause of our sins; wherefore also he called it a fetter, as it can hinder the soul from good works.

III. That if the body was given to the soul after the fall as a fetter, it must have been given as a fetter upon the evil or the good. Now it is impossible that it should be upon the good; for no physician or artificer gives to that which has gone wrong a remedy to cause further error, much less would God do so. It remains, then, that it was a fetter upon evil. But surely we see that, at the beginning,

Cain, clad in this body, committed murder; and it is evident into what wickedness those who succeeded him ran. The body is not, then, a fetter upon evil, nor indeed a fetter at all; nor was the soul clothed in it for the first time after the fall.

IV. That man, with respect to his nature, is most truly said to be neither soul without body, nor, on the other hand, body without soul; but a being composed out of the union of soul and body into one form of the beautiful. But Origen said that the soul alone is man, as did Plato.

V. That there is a difference between man and other living creatures; and to them are given varieties of natural form and shape, as many as the tangible and visible forces of nature produced at the command of God; while to him was given the form and image of God, with every part accurately finished, after the very original likeness of the Father and the only begotten

Son. Now we must consider how the saint states this.

VI. He says that Phidias the statuary, after he had made the Pisæan image of ivory, ordered oil to be poured out before it, that, as far as he could secure it, it might be preserved imperishable.

VII. He says, as was said also by Athenagoras, that the devil is a spirit, made by God, in the neighborhood of matter, as of course the rest of the angels are, and that he was entrusted with the oversight of matter, and the forms of matter. For, according to the original constitution of angels, they were made by God, in His providence, for the care of the universe; in order that, while God exercises a perfect and general supervision over the whole, and keeps the supreme authority and power over all—for upon Him their existence depends—the angels appointed for this purpose take charge of particulars. Now the rest of them remained in the positions for which God made and appointed them; but the devil was insolent, and having conceived envy of us, behaved wickedly in the charge committed to him; as also did those who subsequently were enamored of fleshly charms, and had illicit intercourse with the daughters of men. For to them also, as was the case with men, God granted the possession of their own choice. And how is this to be taken?

VIII. He says that by the coats of skins is signified death. For he says of Adam, that when the Almighty God saw that by treachery he, an immortal being, had become evil, just as his deceiver the devil was, He prepared the coats of skins on this account; that when he was thus, as it were, clothed in mortality, all that was evil in him might die in the dissolution of the body.

IX. He holds that St. Paul had two revelations. For the apostle, he says, does not suppose paradise to be in the third heaven, in the opinion of those who knew how to observe the niceties of language, when he says, "I know such a man caught up to the third heaven; and I know such a man, whether in the body or out of the body, God knows, that was caught up into paradise." Here he signifies that he has seen two revelations, having been evidently taken up twice, once to the third heaven, and once into paradise. For the words, "I know such a man caught up," make it certain that he was personally shown a revelation respecting the third heaven. And the words which follow, "And I know such a man, whether in the body or out of the body, God knows, that he was caught up into paradise," show that another revelation was made to him respecting paradise. Now he was led to make this statement by his opponent's having laid it down from the apostle's words that paradise is a mere conception, as it is above the heaven, in order to draw the conclusion that life in paradise is incorporeal.

X. He says that it is in our power to do, or to avoid doing, evil; since otherwise we should not be punished for doing evil, nor be rewarded for doing well; but the presence or absence of evil thoughts does not depend upon ourselves. Wherefore even the sainted Paul says, "For what I would, that do I not, but what I would not, that I do;" that is to say, "My thoughts are not what I would, but what I would not." Now he says that the habit of imagining evil is rooted out by the approach of physical death,—since it was for this reason that death was appointed by God for the sinner, that evil might not remain forever. But what is the meaning of this statement? It is to be noted that it has been made by others of our Fathers as well. *What is the meaning*, seeing that those who meet death find in it at the time neither increase nor decrease of sins?

II. A Synopsis of Some Apostolic Words from the Same Discourse.

I. Read a compendious interpretation of some apostolic words from the same discourse. Let us see, then, what it is that we have endeavored to say respecting the apostle. For this saying of his, "I was alive without the law once," refers to the life which was lived in paradise before the law, not without a body, but with a body, by our first parents, as we have shown above; for we lived without concupiscence, being altogether ignorant of its assaults. For not to have a law according to which we ought to live, nor a power of establishing what manner of life we ought to adopt, so that we might justly be approved or blamed, is considered to exempt a person from accusation. Because one cannot lust after those things from which he is not restrained, and even if he lusted after them, he would not be blamed. For lust is not directed to things which are before us, and subject to our power, but to those which are before us, and not in our power. For how should one care for a thing which is neither forbidden nor necessary to him? And for this reason it is said, "I had not known lust, except the law had said, Thou shalt not covet." For when (our first parents) heard, "Of the tree of the knowledge of good and evil, thou shalt not eat of it; for in the day thou eats thereof thou shalt surely die," then they conceived lust, and gathered it. Therefore was it said, I had not known lust, except the law had said, Thou shalt not covet;" nor would they have desired to eat, except it had been said, "Thou shalt not eat of it." For it was thence that sin took occasion to deceive me. For when the law was given, the devil had it in his power to work lust in me; "for without the law, sin was dead;" which means "when the law was not given, sin could not be committed." But I was alive and blameless before the law, having no commandment in accordance with which it was necessary to live; "but when the commandment came, sin revived, and I died. And the commandment, which was ordained to life, I found to be unto death." For after God had given the law, and had commanded me what I ought to do, and what I ought not to do, the devil wrought lust in me. For the promise of God which was given to me, this was for life and incorruption, so that obeying it I might have ever-blooming life and joy unto incorruption; but to him who disobeyed it, it would issue in death. But the devil, whom he calls sin, because he is the author of sin, taking occasion by the commandment to deceive me to disobedience, deceived and slew me, thus rendering me subject to the condemnation, "In the day that thou eats thereof thou shalt surely die." "Wherefore the law is holy, and the commandment holy, and just and good;" because it was given, not for injury, but for safety; for let us not suppose that God makes anything useless or hurtful. What then? "Was then that which is good made death unto me?" namely, that which was given as a law, that it might be the cause of the greatest good? "God forbid." For it was not the law of God that became the cause of my being brought into subjection to corruption, but the devil; that he might be made manifested who, through that which is good, wrought evil; that the inventor of evil might become and be proved the greatest of all sinners. "For we know that the law is spiritual;" and therefore it can in no respect be injurious to anyone; for spiritual things are far removed from irrational lust and sin. "But I am carnal, sold under sin;" which means: But I being carnal, and being placed between good and evil as a voluntary agent, am so that I may have it in my power to choose what I will. For "behold I set before thee life and death;" meaning that death would result from disobedience of the spiritual law, that is of the commandment; and from obedience to the carnal law, that is the counsel of the serpent; for by such a choice "I am sold" to the devil, fallen under sin. Hence evil, as though besieging me, cleaves to me and dwells in me, justice giving me up to be sold to the Evil One, in consequence of having violated the law. Therefore also the expressions: "That which I do, I allow not," and "what I hate, that do I," are not to be understood of doing evil, but of only thinking it. For it is not in our power to think or not to think of improper things, but to act or not to act upon our thoughts. For we cannot hinder thoughts from coming into our minds, since we receive them when they are inspired into us from without; but we are able to abstain from obeying them and acting upon them. Therefore it is in our power to will not to think these things; but not to bring it about that they shall pass away, so as not to come into the mind again; for this does not lie in our power, as I said; which is the meaning of that statement, "The good that I would, I do not;" for I do not will to think the things which injure me; for this good is altogether innocent. But "the good that I would, I do not; but the evil which I would not, that I do;" not willing to think, and yet thinking what I do not will. And consider whether it was not for these very things that David entreated God, grieving that he thought of those things which he did not will: "O cleanse Thou me from my secret faults. Keep Thy servant also from presumptuous sins, lest they get the dominion over me; so shall I be undefiled, and innocent from the great offence." And the apostle too, in another place: "Casting down imaginations, and every high thing that exalted itself against the knowledge of God, and bringing into captivity every thought to the obedience of Christ."

II. But if anyone should venture to oppose this statement, and reply, that the apostle teaches that we hate not only the evil which is in thought, but that we do that which we will not, and we hate it even in the very act of doing it, for he says, "The good which I would, I do not; but the evil which I would not, that I do;" if he who says so speaks the truth, let us ask him to explain what was the evil which the apostle hated and willed not to do, but did;

and the good which he willed to do, but did not; and conversely, whether as often as he willed to do good, so often he did not do the good which he willed, but did the evil which he willed not? And how he can say, when exhorting us to shake off all manner of sin, "Be ye followers of me, even as I also am of Christ?" Thus he meant the things already mentioned which he willed not to do, not to be done, but only to be thought of. For how otherwise could he be an exact imitation of Christ? It would be excellent then, and most delightful, if we had not those who oppose us, and contend with us; but since this is impossible, we cannot do what we will. For we will not to have those who lead us to passion, for then we could be saved without weariness and effort; but that does not come to pass which we will, but that which we will not. For it is necessary, as I said, that we should be tried. Let us not then, O my soul, let us not give in to the Evil One; but putting on "the whole armor of God," which is our protection, let us have "the breastplate of righteousness, and your feet shod with the preparation of the Gospel (of peace). Above all, taking the shield of faith, wherewith ye shall be able to quench all the fiery darts of the wicked. And take the helmet of salvation, and the sword of the spirit, which is the Word of God," that ye may be able to stand against the wiles of the devil; "casting down imaginations, and every high thing that exalted itself against the knowledge of Christ," "for we wrestle not against flesh and blood;" "for that which I do, I allow not; for what I would, that do I not: but what I hate, that do I. If then I do that which I would not, I consent unto the law that it is good. Now then it is no more I that do it, but sin that dwelled in me. For I know that in me—that is, in my flesh—dwelled no good thing."

And this is rightly said. For remember how it has been already shown that, from the time when man went astray and disobeyed the law, thence sin, receiving its birth from his disobedience, dwelt in him. For thus a commotion was stirred up, and we were filled with agitations and foreign imaginations, being emptied of the divine inspiration and filled with carnal desire, which the cunning serpent infused into us. And, therefore, God invented death for our sakes, that He might destroy sin, lest rising up in us immortals, as I said, it should be immortal. When the apostle says, "for I know that in me—that is, in my flesh—dwelled no good thing," by which words he means to indicate that sin dwells in us, from the transgression, through lust; out of which, like young shoots, the imaginations of pleasure rise around us. For there are two kinds of thoughts in us; the one which arises from the lust which lies in the body, which, as I said, came from the craft of the Evil Spirit; the other from the law, which is in accordance with the commandment, which we had implanted in us as a natural law, stirring up our thoughts to good, when we delight in the law of God according to our mind, for this is the inner man; but in the law of the devil according to the lust which dwells in the flesh. For he who wars against and opposes the law of God, that is, against the tendency of the mind to good, is the same who stirs up the carnal and sensual impulses to lawlessness.

  III. For the apostle here sets forth clearly, as I think, three laws: One in accordance with the good which is implanted in us, which clearly he calls the law of the mind. One the law which arises from the assault of evil, and which often draws on the soul to lustful fancies, which, he says," wars against the law of the mind." And the third, which is in accordance with sin, settled in the flesh from lust, which he calls the "law of sin which dwells in our members;" which the Evil One, urging on, often stirs up against us, driving us to unrighteousness and evil deeds. For there seems to be in ourselves one thing which is better and another which is worse. And when that which is in its nature better is about to become more powerful than that which is worse, the whole mind is carried on to that which is good; but when that which is worse increases and overbalances, man is on the contrary urged on to evil imaginations. On account of which the apostle prays to be delivered from it, regarding it as death and destruction; as also does the prophet when he says, "Cleanse Thou me from my secret faults." And the same is denoted by the words, "For I delight in the law of God after the inward man; but I see another law in my members, warring against the law of my mind, and bringing me into captivity to the law of sin which is in my members. O wretched man that I am! Who shall deliver me from the body of this death?" By which he does not mean that the body is death, but the law of sin which is in his members, lying hidden in us through the transgression, and ever deluding the soul to the death of unrighteousness. And he immediately adds, clearly showing from what kind of death he desired to be delivered, and who he was who delivered him, "I thank God, through Jesus Christ." And it should be considered, if he said that this body was death, O Aglaophon, as you supposed, he would not afterwards mention Christ as delivering him from so great an evil. For in that case what a strange thing should we have had from the advent of Christ? And how could the apostle have said this, as being able to be delivered from death by the advent of Christ; when it was the lot of all to die before Christ's coming into the world? And, therefore, O Aglaophon, he says not that this body was death, but the sin which dwells in the body through lust, from which God has delivered him by the coming of Christ. "For the law of the Spirit of life in Christ Jesus hath made me free from the law of sin and death;" so that "He that raised up Jesus from the dead shall also quicken your mortal bodies by His Spirit that dwelled in you;" having "condemned sin" which is in the body to its destruction; "that the righteousness of the law" of nature which draws us to good, and is in accordance with the commandment, might be kindled and manifested. For the good which "the law" of nature "could not do, in that it was weak," being overcome by the lust which lies in the body, God gave strength to accomplish, "sending His own Son in the likeness of sinful flesh;" so that sin being condemned, to its destruction, so that it should never bear fruit in the flesh, the righteousness of the law of nature might be fulfilled, abounding in the obedience of those who walk not according to the lust of the flesh, but according to the lust and guidance of the Spirit; "for the law of the Spirit of life," which is the Gospel, being different from earlier laws, leading by its preaching to obedience and the remission of sins, delivered us from the law of sin and death, having conquered entirely sin which reigned over our flesh.

IV. He says that plants are neither nourished nor increased from the earth. For he says, let anyone consider how the earth can be changed and taken up into the substance of trees. For then the place of the earth which lay around, and was drawn up through the roots into the whole compass of the tree, where the tree grew, must needs be hollowed out; so that such a thing as they hold respecting the flux of bodies, is absurd. For how could the earth first enter in through the roots into the trunks of the plants, and then, passing through their channels into all their branches, be turned into leaves and fruit? Now there are large trees, such as the cedar, pines, firs, which annually bear much leaves and fruit; and one may see that they consume none of the surrounding earth into the bulk and substance of the tree. For it would be necessary, if it were true that the earth went up through the roots, and was turned into wood, that the whole place where the earth lay round about them should be hollowed out; for it is not the nature of a dry substance to flow in, like a moist substance, and fill up the place of that which moves away. Moreover, there are fig-trees, and other similar plants, which frequently grow in the buildings of monuments, and yet they never consume the entire building into themselves. But if anyone should choose to collect their fruit and leaves for many years, he would perceive that their bulk had become much larger than the earth upon the monuments. Hence it is absurd to suppose that the earth is consumed into the crop of fruits and leaves; and even if they were all made by it, they would be so only as using it for their seat and place. For bread is not made without a mill, and a place, and time, and fire; and yet bread is not made out of any of these things. And the same may be said of a thousand other things.

V. Now the followers of Origen bring forward this passage, "For we know that if our earthly house of this tabernacle were dissolved," and so forth, to disprove the resurrection of the body, saying that the "tabernacle" is the body, and the "house not made with hands" "in the heavens" is our spiritual clothing. Therefore, says the holy Methodius, by this earthly house must metaphorically be understood our short-lived existence here, and not this tabernacle; for if you decide to consider the body as being the earthly house which is dissolved, tell us what is the tabernacle whose house is dissolved? For the tabernacle is one thing, and the house of the tabernacle another, and still another we who have the tabernacle. "For," he says, "if our earthly house of this tabernacle be dissolved"—by which he points out that the souls are ourselves, that the body is a tabernacle, and that the house of the tabernacle figuratively represents the enjoyment of the flesh in the present life. If, then, this present life of the body be dissolved like a house, we shall have that which is not made with hands in the heavens. "Not made with hands," he says, to point out the difference; because this life may be said to be made with hands, seeing that all the employments and pursuits of life are carried on by the hands of men. For the body, being the workmanship of God, is not said to be made with hands, inasmuch as it is not formed by the arts of men. But if they shall say that it is made with hands, because it was the workmanship of God, then our souls also, and the angels, and the spiritual clothing in the heavens, are made with hands; for all these things, also, are the workmanship of God. What, then, is the house which is made with hands? It is, as I have said, the short-lived existence which is sustained by human hands. For God said, "In the sweat of thy face shalt thou eat bread;" and when that life is dissolved, we have the life which is not made with hands. As also the Lord showed, when He said: "Make to yourselves friends of the mammon of unrighteousness; that, when ye fail, they may receive you into everlasting habitations." For what the Lord then called "habitations," the apostle here calls "clothing." And what He there calls "friends" "of unrighteousness," the apostle here calls "houses" "dissolved." As then, when the days of our present life shall fail, those good deeds of beneficence to which we have attained in this unrighteous life, and in this "world" which "lies in wickedness," will receive our souls; so when this perishable life shall be dissolved, we shall have the habitation which is before the resurrection—that is, our souls shall be with God, until we shall receive the new house which is prepared for us, and which shall never fall. Whence also "we groan," "not for that we would be unclothed," as to the body, "but clothed upon" by it in the other life. For the "house in heaven," with which we desire to be "clothed," is immortality; with which, when we are clothed, every weakness and mortality will be entirely "swallowed up" in it, being consumed by endless life. "For we walk by faith, not by sight;" that is, for we still go forward by faith, viewing the things which are beyond with a darkened understanding, and not clearly, so that we may see these things, and enjoy them, and be in them. "Now this I say, brethren, that flesh and blood cannot inherit the kingdom of God; neither doth corruption inherit incorruption." By flesh, he did not mean flesh itself, but the irrational impulse towards the lascivious pleasures of the soul. And therefore when he says, "Flesh and blood cannot inherit the kingdom of God," he adds the explanation, "Neither doth corruption inherit incorruption." Now corruption is not the thing which is corrupted, but the thing which corrupts. For when death prevails the body sinks into corruption; but when life still remains in it, it stands uncorrupted. Therefore, since the flesh is the boundary between corruption and incorruption, not being either corruption or incorruption, it was vanquished by corruption on account of pleasure, although it was the work and the possession of incorruption. Therefore it became subject to corruption. When, then, it had been overcome by corruption, and was given over to death for chastisement, He did not leave it to be vanquished and given over as an inheritance to corruption; but again conquering death by the resurrection, He restored it to incorruption, that corruption might not inherit incorruption, but incorruption that which is corruptible. And therefore the apostle answers, "This corruptible must put on incorruption, and this mortal immortality." But the corruptible and mortal putting on incorruption and immortality, what else is this, but that which is sown in corruption rising in incorruption? For, "as we have borne the image of the earthly, we shall also bear the image of the heavenly." For the "image of the earthly" which we have borne refers to the saying, "Dust thou art, and unto dust thou shalt return." And the "image of the heavenly is the resurrection from the dead and incorruption."

VI. Now Justin of Neapolis, a man not far removed either from the times or from the virtues of the apostles, says that that which is mortal is inherited, but that life inherits; and that flesh dies, but that the kingdom of heaven lives. When then, Paul says that "flesh and blood cannot inherit the kingdom of heaven," he does not so speak as seeming to slight the regeneration of the flesh, but as teaching that the kingdom of God, which is eternal life, is not inherited by the body, but the body by life. For if the kingdom of God, which is life, were inherited by the body, it would happen that life was swallowed up by corruption. But now life inherits that which is mortal, that death may be swallowed up of life unto victory, and that which is corruptible appear the possession of incorruption; being made free from death and sin, and become the slave and subject of immortality, that the body may become the possession of incorruption, and not incorruption of the body.

VII. Now the passage, "The dead in Christ shall rise first: then we which are alive," St. Methodius thus explains: Those are our bodies; for the souls are we ourselves, who, rising, resume that which is dead from the earth; so that being caught up with them to meet the Lord, we may gloriously celebrate the splendid festival of the resurrection, because we have received our everlasting tabernacles, which shall no longer die nor be dissolved.

VIII. I saw, he says, on Olympus (Olympus is a mountain in Lycia), a fire spontaneously arising on the top of the mountain from the earth, beside which is the plant Puragnos, so flourishing, green, and shady, that it seemed rather as though it grew from a fountain. For what cause, although they are by nature corruptible, and their bodies consumed by fire, was this plant not only not burnt, but rather more flourishing, although in its nature it is easily burnt, and the fire was burning about its roots? Then I cast branches of trees out of the surrounding wood into the place where the fire streamed forth, and, immediately bursting up into flame, they were converted into cinders. What then is the meaning of this contradiction? This God appointed as a sign and prelude of the coming Day that we may know that, when all things are overwhelmed by fire, the bodies which are endowed with chastity and righteousness shall pass through it as though it were cold water.

IX. Consider, he says, whether too the blessed John, when he says, "And the sea gave up the dead which were in it: and death and hell delivered up the dead which were in them," does not mean the parts which are given up by the elements for the reconstruction of each one? By the sea is meant the moist element; by hell, the air, derived from ἀειδές, because it is invisible, as was said by Origen; and by death, the earth, because those who die are laid in it; whence also it is called in the Psalms the "dust of death," Christ saying that He is brought "into the dust of death."

X. For, he says, whatever is composed and consists of pure air and pure fire, and is of like substance with the angelic beings, cannot have the nature of earth and water; since it would then be earthy. And of such nature, and consisting of such things, Origen has shown that the body of man shall be which shall rise, which he also said would be spiritual.

XI. And he asks what will be the appearance of the risen body, when this human form, as according to him useless, shall wholly disappear; since it is the most lovely of all things which are combined in living creatures, as being the form which the Deity Himself employs, as the most wise Paul explains: "For a man indeed ought not to cover his head, forasmuch as he is the image and glory of God;" in accordance with which the rational bodies of the angels are set in order? Will it be circular, or polygonal, or cubical, or pyramidal? For there are very many kinds of forms; but this is impossible. Well then, what are we to think of the assertion, that the godlike shape is to be rejected as more ignoble, for he himself allows that the soul is like the body, and that man is to rise again without hands or feet?

XII. The transformation, he says, is the restoration into an impassible and glorious state. For now the body is a body of desire and of humiliation, and therefore Daniel was called "a man of desires." But then it will be transfigured into an impassible body, not by the change of the arrangement of the members, but by its not desiring carnal pleasures.

Then he says, refuting Origen, Origen therefore thinks that the same flesh will not be restored to the soul, but that the form of each, according to the appearance by which the flesh is now distinguished, shall arise stamped upon another spiritual body; so that everyone will again appear the same form; and that this is the resurrection which is promised. For, he says, the material body being fluid, and in no wise remaining in itself, but wearing out and being replaced around the appearance by which its shape is distinguished, and by which the figure is contained, it is necessary that the resurrection should be only that of the form.

XIII. Then, after a little, he says: If then, O Origen, you maintain that the resurrection of the body changed into a spiritual body is to be expected only in appearance, and put forth the vision of Moses and Elias as a most convincing proof of it; saying that they appeared after their departure from life, preserving no different appearance from that which they had from the beginning; in the same way will be the resurrection of all men. But Moses and Elias arose and appeared with this form of which you speak, before Christ suffered and rose. How then could Christ be celebrated by prophets and apostles as "the first begotten of the dead?" For if the Christ is believed to be the first begotten of the dead, He is the first begotten of the dead as having risen before all others. But Moses appeared to the apostles before Christ suffered, having this form in which you say the resurrection is fulfilled. Hence then, there is no resurrection of the form without the flesh. For either there is a resurrection of the form as you teach, and then Christ is no longer "the first begotten of the dead," from the fact that souls appeared before Him, having this form after death; or He is truly the first begotten, and it is quite impossible that any should have been thought meet for a resurrection before Him, so as not to die again. But if no one arose before Him, and Moses and Elias appeared to the apostles not having flesh, but only its appearance, the resurrection in the flesh is clearly manifested. For it is most absurd that the resurrection should be set forth only in form, since the souls, after their departure from the flesh, never appear to lay aside the form which, he says, rises again. But if that remains with them, so that it cannot be taken away, as with the soul of Moses and Elias; and neither perishes, as you think, nor is destroyed, but is everywhere present with them; then surely that form which never fell cannot be said to rise again.

XIV. But if anyone, finding this inadmissible, answers, But how then, if no one rose before Christ went down into Hades, are several recorded as having risen before Him? Among whom is the son of the widow of Sarepta, and the son of the Shunammite, and Lazarus. We must say: These rose to die again; but we are speaking of those who shall never die after their rising. And if anyone should speak doubtfully concerning the soul of Elias, as that the Scriptures say that he was taken up in the flesh, and we say that he appeared to the apostles divested of the flesh, we must say, that to allow that he appeared to the apostles in the flesh is more in favor of our argument. For it is shown by this case that the body is susceptible of immortality, as was also proved by the translation of Enoch. For if he could not receive immortality, he could not remain in a state of insensibility so long a time. If, then, he appeared with the body, that was truly after he was dead, but certainly not as having arisen from the dead. And this, we may say, if we agree with Origen when he says that the same form is given to the soul after death; when it is separated from the body, which is of all things the most impossible, from the fact that the form of the flesh was destroyed before by its changes, as also the form of the melted statue before its entire dissolution. Because the quality cannot be separated from the material, so as to exist by itself; for the shape which disappears around the brass is separated from the melted statue, and has not longer a substantial existence.

XV. Since the form is said to be separated in death from the flesh, come, let us consider in how many ways that which is separated is said to be separated. Now a thing is said to be separated from another either in act and subsistence, or in thought; or else in act, but not in subsistence. As if, for instance, one should separate from each other wheat and barley which had been mingled together; in as far as they are separated in motion, they are said to be separated in act; in as far as they stand apart when separated, they are said to be separated in subsistence. They are separated in thought when we separate matter from its qualities, and qualities from matter; in act, but not in subsistence, when a thing separated from another no longer exists, not having a substantive existence. And it may be observed that it is so also in mechanics, when one looks upon a statue or a brazen horse melted. For, when he considers these things, he will see their natural form changing; and they alter into another figure from which the original form disappears. For if anyone should melt down the works formed into the semblance of a man or a horse, he will find the appearance of the form disappearing, but the material itself remaining. It is, therefore, untenable to say, that the form shall arise in nowise corrupted, but that the body in which the form was stamped shall be destroyed.

XVI. But he says that it will be so; for it will be changed in a spiritual body. Therefore, it is necessary to confess that the very same form as at first does not arise, from its being changed and corrupted with the flesh. For although it be changed into a spiritual body, that will not be properly the original substance, but a certain resemblance of it, fashioned in an ethereal body. If, however, it is not the same form, nor yet the body which arises, then it is another in the place of the first. For that which is like, being different from that which it resembles, cannot be that very first thing in accordance with which it was made.

XVII. Moreover, he says that that is the appearance or form which shows forth the identity of the members in the distinctive character of the form.

XVIII. And, when Origen allegorizes that which is said by the prophet Ezekiel concerning the resurrection of the dead, and perverts it to the return of the Israelites from their captivity in Babylon, the saint in refuting him, after many other remarks, says this also: For neither did they obtain a perfect liberty, nor did they overcome their enemies by a greater power, and dwell again in Jerusalem; and when they frequently intended to build (the temple), they were prevented by other nations. Whence, also, they were scarce able to build that in forty six years, which Solomon completed from the foundations in seven years. But what need we say on this subject? For from the time of Nebuchadnezzar, and those who after him reigned over Babylon, until the time of the Persian expedition against the Assyrians, and the empire of Alexander, and the war which was stirred up by the Romans against the Jews, Jerusalem was six times overthrown by its enemies. And this is recorded by Josephus, who says: "Jerusalem was taken in the second year of the reign of Vespasian. It had been taken before five times; but now for the second time it was destroyed. For Asochæus, king of Egypt, and after him Antiochus, next Pompey, and after these Sosius, with Herod, took the city and burnt it; but before these, the king of Babylon conquered and destroyed it."

XIX. He says that Origen holds these opinions which he refutes. And there may be a doubt concerning Lazarus and the rich man. The simpler persons think that these things were spoken as though both were receiving their due for the things which they had done in life in their bodies; but the more accurate think that, since no one is left in life after the resurrection, these things do not happen at the resurrection. For the rich man says: "I have five brethren;...lest they also come into this place of torment," send Lazarus, that he may tell them of those things which are here. And, therefore, if we ask respecting the "tongue," and the "finger," and "Abraham's bosom," and the reclining there, it may perhaps be that the soul receives in the change a form similar in appearance to its gross and earthly body. If, then, any one of those who have fallen asleep is recorded as having appeared, in the same way he has been seen in the form which he had when he was in the flesh. Besides, when Samuel appeared, it is clear that, being seen, he was clothed in a body; and this must especially be admitted, if we are pressed by arguments which prove that the essence of the soul is incorporeal, and is manifested by itself. But the rich man in torment, and the poor man who was comforted in the bosom of Abraham, are said, the one to be punished in Hades, and the other to be comforted in Abraham's bosom, before the appearing of the Savior, and before the end of the world, and therefore before the resurrection; teaching that now already, at the change, the soul rises a body. Wherefore, the saint says as follows: Setting forth that the soul, after its removal hence, has a form similar in appearance to this sensitive body; does Origen represent the soul, after Plato, as being incorporeal? And how should that which, after removal from the world, is said to have need of a vehicle and a clothing, so that it might not be found naked, be in itself other than incorporeal? But if it be incorporeal, must it not also be incapable of passion? For it follows, from its being incorporeal, that it is also impassible and imperturbable. If, then, it was not distracted by any irrational desire, neither was it changed by a pained or suffering body. For neither can that which is incorporeal sympathize with a body, nor a body with that which is incorporeal, if, indeed, the soul should seem to be incorporeal, in accordance with what has been said. But if it sympathize with the body, as is proved by the testimony of those who appear, it cannot be incorporeal. Therefore God alone is celebrated, as the unbegotten, independent, and unwearied nature; being incorporeal, and therefore invisible; for "no man hath seen God." But souls, being rational bodies, are arranged by the Maker and Father of all things into members which are visible to reason, having received this impression. Whence, also, in Hades, as in the case of Lazarus and the rich man, they are spoken of as having a tongue, and a finger, and the other members; not as though they had with them another invisible body, but that the souls themselves, naturally, when entirely stripped of their covering, are such according to their essence.

XX. The saint says at the end: The words, "For to this end Christ both died, and rose, and revived, that He might be Lord both of the dead and living," must be taken as referring to souls and bodies; the souls being the *living*, as being immortal, and the bodies being *dead*.

XXI. Since the body of man is more honorable than other living creatures, because it is said to have been formed by the hands of God, and because it has attained to be the vehicle of the reasonable soul; how is it that it is so short-lived, shorter even than some of the irrational creatures? Is it not clear that its long-lived existence will be after the resurrection?

Fragments.

On the History of Jonah.
From the Book on the Resurrection.

I. The history of Jonah contains a great mystery. For it seems that the whale signifies Time, which never stands still, but is always going on, and consumes the things which are made by long and shorter intervals. But Jonah, who fled from the presence of God, is himself the first man who, having transgressed the law, fled from being seen naked of immortality, having lost through sin his confidence in the Deity. And the ship in which he embarked, and which was tempest-tossed, is this brief and hard life in the present time; just as though we had turned and removed from that blessed and secure life, to that which was most tempestuous and unstable, as from solid land to a ship. For what a ship is to the land, that our present life is to that which is immortal. And the storm and the tempests which beat against us are the temptations of this life, which in the world, as in a tempestuous sea, do not permit us to have a fair voyage free from pain, in a calm sea, and one which is free from evils. And the casting of Jonah from the ship into the sea, signifies the fall of the first man from life to death, who received that sentence because, through having sinned, he fell from righteousness: "Dust thou art, and unto dust shalt thou return." And his being swallowed by the whale signifies our inevitable removal by time. For the belly in which Jonah, when he was swallowed, was concealed, is the all-receiving earth, which receives all things which are consumed by time.

II. As, then, Jonah spent three days and as many nights in the whale's belly, and was delivered up sound again, so shall we all, who have passed through the three stages of our present life on earth—I mean the beginning, the middle, and the end, of which all this present time consists—rise again. For there are altogether three intervals of time, the past, the future, and the present. And for this reason the Lord spent so many days in the earth symbolically, thereby teaching clearly that when the aforementioned intervals of time have been fulfilled, then shall come our resurrection, which is the beginning of the future age, and the end of this. For in that age there is neither past nor future, but only the present. Moreover, Jonah having spent three days and three nights in the belly of the whale, was not destroyed by his flesh being dissolved, as is the case with that natural decomposition which takes place in the belly, in the case of those meats which enter into it, on account of the greater heat in the liquids, that it might be shown that these bodies of ours may remain undestroyed. For consider that God had images of Himself made as of gold, that is of a purer spiritual substance, as the angels; and others of clay or brass, as ourselves. He united the soul which was made in the image of God to that which was earthy. As, then, we must here honor all the images of a king, on account of the form which is in them, so also it is incredible that we who are the images of God should be altogether destroyed as being without honor. Whence also the Word descended into our world, and was incarnate of our body, in order that, having fashioned it to a more divine image, He might raise it incorrupt, although it had been dissolved by time. And, indeed, when we trace out the dispensation which was figuratively set forth by the prophet, we shall find the whole discourse visibly extending to this.

Extracts from the Work on Things Created.

I. This selection is made, by way of compendium or synopsis, from the work of the holy martyr and bishop Methodius, concerning things created. The passage, "Give not that which is holy unto the dogs, neither cast ye your pearls before swine," is explained by Origen as signifying that the pearls are the more mystical teachings of our God-given religion, and the swine those who roll in impiety and in all kinds of pleasures, as swine do in mud; for he said that it was taught by these words of Christ not to cast about the divine teachings, inasmuch as they could not bear them who were held by impiety and brutal pleasures. The great Methodius says: If we must understand by pearls the glorious and divine teachings, and by swine those who are given up to impiety and pleasures, from whom are to be withheld and hidden the apostle's teachings, which stir men up to piety and faith in Christ, see how you say that no Christians can be converted from their impiety by the teachings of the apostles. For they would never cast the mysteries of Christ to those who, through want of faith, are like swine. Either, therefore, these things were cast before all the Greeks and other unbelievers, and were preached by the disciples of Christ, and converted them from impiety to the faith of Christ, as we believers certainly confess, and then the words, "Cast not your pearls before swine," can no longer mean what has been said; or meaning this, we must say that faith in Christ and deliverance from impiety have been accorded to none of the unbelievers, whom we compare to swine, by the apostolic instructions enlightening their souls like pearls. But this is blasphemous. Therefore the pearls in this place are not to be taken to mean the deepest doctrines, and the swine the impious; nor are we to understand the words, "Cast not your pearls before swine," as forbidding us to cast before the impious and unbelieving the deep and sanctifying doctrines of faith in Christ; but we must take the pearls to mean virtues, with which the soul is adorned as with precious pearls; and not to cast them before swine, as meaning that we are not to cast these virtues, such as chastity, temperance, righteousness, and truth, that we are not to cast these to impure pleasures, for these are like swine, lest they, fleeing from the virtues, cause the soul to live a swinish and a vicious life.

II. Origen says that what he calls the Centaur is the universe which is co-eternal with the only wise and independent God. For he says, since there is no workman without some work, or maker without something made, so neither is there an Almighty without an object of His power. For the workman must be so called from his work, and the maker from what he makes, and the Almighty

Ruler from that which He rules over. And so it must be, that these things were made by God from the beginning, and that there was no time in which they did not exist. For if there was a time when the things that are made did not exist, then, as there were no things which had been made, so there was no maker; which you see to be an impious conclusion. And it will result that the unchangeable and unaltered God has altered and changed. For if He made the universe later, it is clear that He passed from not making to making. But this is absurd in connection with what has been said. It is impossible, therefore, to say that the universe is not unbeginning and co-eternal with God. To whom the saint replies, in the person of another, asking, "Do you not consider God the beginning and fountain of wisdom and glory, and in short of all virtue in substance and not by acquisition?" "Certainly," he says. "And what besides? Is He not by Himself perfect and independent?" "True; for it is impossible that he who is independent should have his independence from another. For we must say, that all which is full by another is also imperfect. For it is the thing which has its completeness of itself, and in itself alone, which can alone be considered perfect." "You say most truly. For would you pronounce that which is neither by itself complete, nor its own completeness, to be independent?" "By no means. For that which is perfect through anything else must needs be in itself imperfect." "Well, then shall God be considered perfect by Himself, and not by some other?" "Most rightly." "Then God is something different from the world, and the world from God?" "Quite so." "We must not then say that God is perfect, and Creator, and Almighty, through the world?" "No; for He must surely by Himself, and not by the world, and that changeable, be found perfect by Himself." "Quite so." "But you will say that the rich man is called rich on account of his riches? And that the wise man is called wise not as being wisdom itself, but as being a possessor of substantial wisdom?" "Yes." "Well, then, since God is something different from the world, shall He be called on account of the world rich, and beneficent, and Creator?" "By no means. Away with such a thought!" "Well, then, He is His own riches, and is by Himself rich and powerful." "So it seems." "He was then before the world altogether independent, being Father, and Almighty, and Creator; so that He by Himself, and not by another, was this." "It must be so." "Yes; for if He were acknowledged to be Almighty on account of the world, and not of Himself, being distinct from the world,—may God forgive the words, which the necessity of the argument requires,—He would by Himself be imperfect and have need of these things, through which He is marvelously Almighty and Creator. We must not then admit this pestilent sin of those who say concerning God, that He is Almighty and Creator by the things which He controls and creates, which are changeable, and that He is not so by Himself."

III. Now consider it thus: "If, you say, the world was created later, not existing before, then we must change the passionless and unchangeable God; for it must needs be, that he who did nothing before, but afterwards, passes from not doing to doing, changes and is altered." Then I said, "Did God rest from making the world, or not?" "He rested." "Because otherwise it would not have been completed." "True." "If, then, the act of making, after not making, makes an alteration in God, does not His ceasing to make after making the same?" "Of necessity." "But should you say that He is altered as not doing to-day, from what He was, when He was doing?" "By no means. There is no necessity for His being changed, when He makes the world from what He was when He was not making it; and neither is there any necessity for saying that the universe must have co-existed with Him, on account of our not being forced to say that He has changed, nor that the universe is co-eternal with Him."

IV. But speak to me thus: "Should you call that a thing created which had no beginning of its creation?" "Not at all." "But if there is no beginning of its creation, it is of necessity uncreated. But if it was created, you will grant that it was created by some cause. For it is altogether impossible that it should have a beginning without a cause." "It is impossible." "Shall we say, then, that the world and the things which are in it, having come into existence and formerly not existing, are from any other cause than God?" "It is plain that they are from God." "Yes; for it is impossible that that which is limited by an existence which has a beginning should be co-existent with the infinite." "It is impossible." "But again, O Centaur, let us consider it from the beginning. Do you say that the things which exist were created by Divine knowledge or not?" "Oh, be gone, they will say; not at all." "Well, but was it from the elements, or from matter, or the firmaments, or however you choose to name them, for it makes no difference; these things existing beforehand uncreated and borne along in a state of chaos; did God separate them and reduce them all to order, as a good painter who forms one picture out of many colors?" "No, nor yet this." For they will quite avoid making a concession against themselves, lest agreeing that there was a beginning of the separation and transformation of matter, they should be forced in consistency to say, that in all things God began the ordering and adorning of matter which hitherto had been without form.

V. But come now, since by the favor of God we have arrived at this point in our discourse; let us suppose a beautiful statue standing upon its base; and that those who behold it, admiring its harmonious beauty, differ among themselves, some trying to make out that it had been made, others that it had not. I should ask them: For what reason do you say that it was not made? On account of the artist, because he must be considered as never resting from his work? Or on account of the statue itself? If it is on account of the artist, how could it, as not being made, be fashioned by the artist? But if, when it is molded of brass, it has all that is needed in order that it may receive whatever impression the artist chooses, how can that be said not to be made which submits to and receives his labor? If, again, the statue is declared to be by itself perfect and not made, and to have no need of art, then we must allow, in accordance with that pernicious heresy, that it is self-made. If perhaps they are unwilling to admit this argument, and reply more inconsistently, that they do not say that the figure was not made, but that it was always made, so that there was no beginning of its being made, so that artist might be said to have this subject of his art without any beginning. Well then, my friends, we will say to them, if no time, nor any age before can be found in the past, when the statue was not perfect, will you tell us what the artist contributed to it, or wrought upon it? For if this statue has need of nothing, and has no beginning of existence, for this reason, according to you, a maker never made it, nor will any maker be found. And so the argument seems to come again to the same conclusion, and we must allow that it is self-made. For if an artificer is said to have moved a statue ever so slightly, he will submit to a beginning, when he began to move and adorn that which was before unadorned and unmoved. But the world neither was nor will be forever the same. Now we must compare the artificer to God, and the statue to the world. But how then, O foolish men, can you imagine the creation to be co-eternal with its Artificer, and to have no need of an artificer? For it is of necessity that the co-eternal should never have had a beginning of being, and should be equally uncreated and powerful with Him. But the uncreated appears to be in itself perfect and unchangeable, and it will have need of nothing, and be free from corruption. And if this be so, the world can no longer be, as you say it is, capable of change.

VI. He says that the Church is so called from being called out with respect to pleasures.

VII. The saint says: We said there are two kinds of formative power in what we have now acknowledged; the one which works by itself what it chooses, not out of things which already exist, by its bare will, without delay, as soon as it wills. This is the power of the Father. The other which adorns and embellishes, by imitation of the former, the things which already exist. This is the power of the Son, the almighty and powerful hand of the Father, by which, after creating matter not out of things which were already in existence, He adorns it.

VIII. The saint says that the Book of Job is by Moses. He says, concerning the words, "In the beginning God created the heaven and the earth," that one will not err who says that the "Beginning" is Wisdom. For Wisdom is said by one of the Divine band to speak in this manner concerning herself: "The Lord created me the beginning of His ways for His works: of old He laid my foundation." It was fitting and more seemly that all things which came into existence, should be more recent than Wisdom, since they existed through her. Now consider whether the saying: "In the beginning was the Word, and the Word was with God, and the Word was God. The same was in the beginning with God;"—whether these statements be not in agreement with those. For we must say that the Beginning, out of which the most upright Word came forth, is the Father and Maker of all things, in whom it was. And the words, "The same was in the beginning with God," seem to indicate the position of authority of the Word, which He had with the Father before the world came into existence; "beginning" signifying His power. And so, after the peculiar unbeginning beginning, who is the Father, He is the beginning of other things, by whom all things are made.

IX. He says that Origen, after having fabled many things concerning the eternity of the universe, adds this also: Nor yet from Adam, as some say, did man, previously not existing, first take his existence and come into the world. Nor again did the world begin to be made six days before the creation of Adam. But if anyone should prefer to differ in these points, let him first say, whether a period of time be not easily reckoned from the creation of the world, according to the Book of Moses, to those who so receive it, the voice of prophecy here proclaiming: "Thou art God from everlasting, and world without end....For a thousand years in Thy sight are but as yesterday: seeing that is past as a watch in the night." For when a thousand years are reckoned as one day in the sight of God, and from the creation of the world to His rest is six days, so also to our time, six days are defined, as those say who are clever arithmeticians. Therefore, they say that an age of six thousand years extends from Adam to our time. For they say that the judgment will come on the seventh day, that is in the seventh thousand years. Therefore, all the days from our time to that which was in the beginning, in which God created the heaven and the earth, are computed to be thirteen days; before which God, because he had as yet created nothing according to their folly, is stripped of His name of Father and Almighty. But if there are thirteen days in the sight of God from the creation of the world, how can Wisdom say, in the Book of the Son of Sirach: "Who can number the sand of the sea, and the drops of rain, and the days of eternity?" This is what Origen says seriously, and mark how he trifles.

From the Works of Methodius Against Porphyry.
I.
This, in truth, must be called most excellent and praiseworthy, which God Himself considers excellent, even if it be despised and scoffed at by all. For things are not what men think them to be.
II.2977
Then repentance effaces every sin, when there is no delay after the fall of the soul, and the disease is not suffered to go on through a long interval. For then evil will not have power to leave its mark in us, when it is drawn up at the moment of its being set down like a plant newly planted.
III.
In truth, our evil comes out of our want of resemblance to God, and our ignorance of Him; and, on the other hand, our great good consists in our resemblance to Him. And, therefore, our conversion and faith in the

Being who is incorruptible and divine, seems to be truly our proper good, and ignorance and disregard of Him our evil; if, at least, those things which are produced in us and of us, being the evil effects of sin, are to be considered ours.

From His Discourse Concerning Martyrs.

For martyrdom is so admirable and desirable, that the Lord, the Son of God Himself, honoring it, testified, "He thought it not robbery to be equal with God," that He might honor man to whom He descended with this gift.

General Note.

The *Banquet* appears to me a genuine work, although, like other writings of this Father, it may have been corrupted. Tokens of such corruptions are not wanting, and there can be little doubt that Methodius the monkish artist and missionary of the ninth century has been often copied into the works of his earlier namesake.

In a fragment, for example, found on a preceding page, there is a passage on God's image in angels and men, which appears in its more probable form in another fragment, discovered by Combefis. As quoted by St. John Damascene, it is enough to say of it, with the candid Dupin, "*I very much question whether the passage belongs to Methodius*; or, if it does, it must be taken in another sense than that in which Damascene understood it, as the words which immediately precede seem to intimate." That it is a positive *anachronism* in any other sense, is proved by the history of Images, on which see Epiphanius, quoted by Faber, *Difficulties of Romanism*, p. 488, ed. 1830. He gives St. Jerome, *Opp.*, ii. p. 177. A learned friend suggests that the Rev. J. Endell Tyler's popular work on *Primitive Christian Worship* may supply an accessible reference. It is a very good thought, for the whole book is worth reading, on other points also.

> Oration Concerning Simeon and Anna
> On the Day that They Met in the Temple.
> _____

I. Although I have before, as briefly as possible, in my dialogue on chastity, sufficiently laid the foundations, as it were, for a discourse on virginity, yet to-day the season has brought forward the entire subject of the glory of virginity, and its incorruptible crown, for the delightful consideration of the Church's foster-children. For to-day the council chamber of the divine oracles is opened wide, and the signs prefiguring this glorious day, with its effects and issues, are by the sacred preachers read over to the assembled Church. Today the accomplishment of that ancient and true counsel is, in fact and deed, gloriously manifested to the world. Today, without any covering, and with unveiled face, we see, as in a mirror, the glory of the Lord, and the majesty of the divine ark itself. To-day, the most holy assembly, bearing upon its shoulders the heavenly joy that was for generations expected, imparts it to the race of man. "Old things are passed away"—things new burst forth into flowers, and such as fade not away. No longer does the stern decree of the law bear sway, but the grace of the Lord reigns, drawing all men to itself by saving long-suffering. No second time is an Uzziah invisibly punished, for daring to touch what may not be touched; for God Himself invites, and who will stand hesitating with fear? He says: "Come unto Me, all ye that labor and are heavy laden." Who, then, will not run to

Him? Let no Jew contradict the truth, looking at the type which went before the house of Obededom. The Lord has *"manifestly come to His own."* And sitting on a living and not inanimate ark, as upon the mercy-seat, He comes forth in solemn procession upon the earth. The publican, when he touches this ark, comes away just; the harlot, when she approaches this, is remolded, as it were, and becomes chaste; the leper, when he touches this, is restored whole without pain. It repulses none; it shrinks from none; it imparts the gifts of healing, without itself contracting any disease; for the Lord, who loves and cares for man, in it makes His resting-place. These are the gifts of this new grace. This is that new and strange thing that has happened under the sun—a thing that never had place before, nor will have place again. That which God of His compassion toward us foreordained has come to pass, He hath given it fulfilment because of that love for man which is so becoming to Him. With good right, therefore, has the sacred trumpet sounded, "Old things are passed away, behold all things are become new." And what shall I conceive, what shall I speak worthy of this day? I am struggling to reach the inaccessible, for the remembrance of this holy virgin far transcends all words of mine. Wherefore, since the greatness of the panegyric required completely puts to shame our limited powers, let us betake ourselves to that hymn which is not beyond our faculties, and boasting in our own unalterable defeat, let us join the rejoicing chorus of Christ's flock, who are keeping holy-day. And do you, my divine and saintly auditors, keep strict silence, in order that through the narrow channel of ears, as into the harbour of the understanding, the vessel freighted with truth may peacefully sail. We keep festival, not according to the vain customs of the Greek mythology; we keep a feast which brings with it no ridiculous or frenzied banqueting of the gods, but which teaches us the wondrous condescension to us men of the awful glory of Him who is God over all.

II. Come, therefore, Isaiah, most solemn of preachers and greatest of prophets, wisely unfold to the Church the mysteries of the congregation in glory, and incite our excellent guests abundantly, to satiate themselves with enduring dainties, in order that, placing the reality which we possess over against that mirror of thine, truthful prophet as thou art, thou may joyfully clap thine hands at the issue of thy predictions. It came to pass, he says, "in the year in which king Uzziah died, I saw the Lord sitting upon a throne, high and lifted up; and the house was full of His glory. And the seraphim stood round about him: each one had six wings. And one cried unto another, and said, Holy, holy, holy, is the Lord of hosts: the whole earth is full of His glory. And the posts of the door were moved at the voice of him that cried, and the house was filled with smoke. And I said, Woe is me! I am pricked to the heart, for I am a man of unclean lips, and I dwell in the midst of a people of unclean lips: for mine eyes have seen the King, the Lord of hosts. And one of the seraphim was sent unto me, having a live coal in his hand, which he had taken with the tongs from off the altar. And he touched my mouth, and said, Lo, this hath touched thy lips; and thine iniquity is taken away, and thy sin is purged. Also I heard the voice of the Lord, saying, Whom shall I send, and who will go unto this people? Then said I, Here am I; send me. And He said, Go, and tell this people, Hear ye indeed, but understand not; and see ye indeed, but perceive not." These are the proclamations made beforehand by the prophet through the Spirit. Do thou, dearly beloved, consider the force of these words. So shalt thou understand the issue of these sacramental symbols, and know both what and how great this assembling together of ourselves is. And since the prophet has before spoken of this miracle, come thou, and with the greatest ardor and exultation, and alacrity of heart, together with the keenest sagacity of thine intelligence, and therewith approach Bethlehem the renowned, and place before thy mind an image clear and distinct, comparing the prophecy with the actual issue of events. Thou wilt not stand in need of many words to come to a knowledge of the matter; only fix thine eyes on the things which are taking place there. "All things truly are plain to them that understand, and right to them that find knowledge." For, behold, as a throne high and lifted up by the glory of Him that fashioned it, the virgin-mother is there made ready, and that most evidently for the King, the Lord of hosts. Upon this, consider the Lord now coming unto thee in sinful flesh. Upon this virginal throne, I say, worship Him who now comes to thee by this new and ever-adorable way. Look around thee with the eye of faith, and thou wilt find around Him, as by the ordinance of their courses, the royal and priestly company of the seraphim. These, as His bodyguard, are ever wont to attend the presence of their king. Whence also in this place they are not only said to hymn with their praises the divine substance of the divine unity, but also the glory to be adored by all of that one of the sacred Trinity, which now, by the appearance of God in the flesh, hath even lighted upon earth. They say: "The whole earth is full of His glory." For we believe that, together with the Son, who was made man for our sakes, according to the good pleasure of His will, was also present the Father, who is inseparable from Him as to His divine nature, anal also the Spirit, who is of one and the same essence with Him. For, as says Paul, the interpreter of the divine oracle, "God was in Christ reconciling the world unto Himself, not imputing their trespasses unto them." He thus shows that the Father was in the Son, because that one and the same will worked in them.

    III. Do thou, therefore, O lover of this festival, when thou hast considered well the glorious mysteries of Bethlehem, which were brought to pass for thy sake, gladly join thyself to the heavenly host, which is celebrating magnificently thy salvation. As once David did before the ark, so do thou, before this virginal throne, joyfully lead the dance. Hymn with gladsome song the Lord, who is always and everywhere present, and Him who from Teman, as says the prophet, hath thought fit to appear, and that in the flesh, to the race of men. Say, with Moses, "He is my God, and I will glorify Him; my father's God, and I will exalt Him." Then, after thine hymn of thanksgiving, we shall usefully inquire what cause aroused the King of Glory to appear in Bethlehem. His compassion for us compelled Him, who cannot be compelled, to be born in a human body at Bethlehem. But what necessity was there that He, when a suckling infant, that He who, though both in time, was not limited by time, that He, who though wrapped in swaddling clothes, was not by them held fast, what necessity was there that He should be an exile and a stranger from His country? Should you, forsooth, wish to know this, ye congregation most holy, and upon whom the Spirit of God hath breathed, listen to Moses proclaiming plainly to the people, stimulating them, as it were, to the knowledge of this extraordinary nativity, and saying, "Every male that opened the womb, shall be called holy to the Lord." O wondrous circumstance! "O the depth of the riches both of the wisdom and knowledge of God!" It became indeed the Lord of the law and the prophets to do all things in accordance with His own law, and not to make void the law, but to fulfil it, and rather to connect with the fulfilment of the law the beginning of His grace. Therefore it is that the mother, who was superior to the law, submits to the law. And she, the holy and undefiled one, observes that time of forty days that was appointed for the unclean. And He who makes us free from the law, became subject to the law; and there is offered for Him, who hath sanctified us, a pair of clean birds, in testimony of those who approach clean and blameless. Now that that parturition was unpolluted, and stood not in need of expiatory victims, Isaiah is our witness, who proclaims distinctly to the whole earth under the sun: "Before she travailed," he says, "she brought forth; before her pains came, she escaped, and brought forth a man-child." Who hath heard such a thing? Who hath seen such things? The must holy virgin mother, therefore, escaped entirely the manner of women even before she brought forth: doubtless, in order that the Holy Spirit, betrothing her unto Himself, and sanctifying her, she might conceive without intercourse with man. She hath brought forth her first-born Son, even the only-begotten Son of God, Him, I say, who in the heavens above shone forth as the only-begotten, without mother, from out His Father's substance, and preserved the virginity of His natural unity undivided and inseparable; and who on earth, in the virgin's nuptial chamber, joined to Himself the nature of Adam, like a bridegroom, by an inalienable union, and preserved His mother's purity uncorrupt and uninjured—Him, in short, who in heaven was begotten without corruption, and on earth brought forth in a manner quite unspeakable. But to return to our subject.

IV. Therefore the prophet brought the virgin from Nazareth, in order that she might give birth at Bethlehem to her salvation-bestowing child, and brought her back again to Nazareth, in order to make manifest to the world the hope of life. Hence it was that the ark of God removed from the inn at Bethlehem, for there He paid to the law that debt of the forty days, due not to justice but to grace, and rested upon the mountains of Sion, and receiving into His pure bosom as upon a lofty throne, and one transcending the nature of man, the Monarch of all, she presented Him there to God the Father, as the joint-partner of His throne and inseparable from His nature, together with that pure and undefiled flesh which he had of her substance assumed. The holy mother goes up to the temple to exhibit to the law a new and strange wonder, even that child long expected, who opened the virgin's womb, and yet did not burst the barriers of virginity; that child, superior to the law, who yet fulfilled the law; that child that was at once before the law, and yet after it; that child, in short, who was of her incarnate beyond the law of nature. For in other cases every womb being first opened by connection with a man, and, being impregnated by his seed, receives the beginning of conception, and by the pangs which make perfect parturition, doth at length bring forth to light its offspring endowed with reason, and with its nature consistent, in accordance with the wise provision of God its Creator. For God said, "Be fruitful, and multiply, and replenish the earth." But the womb of this virgin, without being opened before, or being impregnated with seed, gave birth to an offspring that transcended nature, while at the same time it was cognate to it, and that without detriment to the indivisible unity, so that the miracle was the more stupendous, the prerogative of virginity likewise remaining intact. She goes up, therefore to the temple, she who was more exalted than the temple, clothed with a double glory—the glory, I say, of undefiled virginity, and that of ineffable fecundity, the benediction of the law, and the sanctification of grace. Wherefore he says who saw it: "And the whole house was full of His glory, and the seraphim stood round about him; and one cried unto another, and said, Holy, holy, holy, is the Lord of hosts: the whole earth is full of His glory." As also the blessed prophet Habakkuk has charmingly sung, saying, "In the midst of two living creatures thou shalt be known: as the years draw nigh thou shalt be recognized—when the time is come thou shalt be shown forth." See, I pray you, the exceeding accuracy of the Spirit. He speaks of knowledge, recognition, showing forth. As to the first of these: "In the midst of two living creatures thou shalt be known," he refers to that overshadowing of the divine glory which, in the time of the law, rested in the Holy of holies upon the covering of the ark, between the typical cherubim, as He says to Moses, "There will I be known to thee." But He refers likewise to that concourse of angels, which hath now come to meet us, by the divine and ever adorable manifestation of the Savior Himself in the flesh, although He in His very nature cannot be beheld by us, as Isaiah has even before declared. But when He says, "As the years draw nigh, thou shalt be recognized," He means, as has been said before, that glorious recognition of our Savior, God in the flesh, who is otherwise invisible to mortal eye; as somewhere Paul, that great interpreter of sacred mysteries, says: "But when the fullness of the time was come, God sent forth His Son, made of a woman, made under the law, to redeem them that were under the law, that we might receive the adoption of sons." And then, as to that which is subjoined, "When the time is come, Thou shalt be shown forth," what exposition doth this require, if a man diligently direct the eye of his mind to the festival which we are now celebrating? "For then shalt Thou be shown forth," He says, "as upon a kingly charger, by Thy pure and chaste mother, in the temple, and that in the grace and beauty of the flesh assumed by Thee." All these things the prophet, summing up for the sake of greater clearness, exclaims in brief: "The Lord is in His holy temple;" "Fear before Him all the earth."

V. Tremendous, verily, is the mystery connected with thee, O virgin mother, thou spiritual throne, glorified and made worthy of God. Thou hast brought forth, before the eyes of those in heaven and earth, a pre-eminent wonder. And it is a proof of this, and an irrefragable argument, that at the novelty of thy supernatural child-bearing, the angels sang on earth, "Glory to God in the highest, and on earth peace, good-will towards men," by their threefold song bringing in a threefold holiness. Blessed art thou among the generations of women, O thou of God most blessed, for by thee the earth has been filled with that divine glory of God; as in the Psalms it is sung: "Blessed be the Lord God of Israel, and the whole earth shall be filled with His glory. Amen. Amen." And the posts of the door, says the prophet, moved at the voice of him that cried, by which is signified the veil of the temple drawn before the ark of the covenant, which typified thee, that the truth might be laid open to me, and also that I might be taught, by the types and figures which went before, to approach with reverence and trembling to do honor to the sacred mystery which is connected with thee; and that by means of this prior shadow-painting of the law I might be restrained from boldly and irreverently contemplating with fixed gaze Him who, in His incomprehensibility, is seated far above all. For if to the ark, which was the image and type of thy sanctity, such honor was paid of God that to no one but to the priestly order only was the access to it open, or ingress allowed to behold it, the veil separating it off, and keeping the vestibule as that of a queen, what, and what sort of veneration is due to thee from us who are of creation the least, to thee who art indeed a queen; to thee, the living ark of God, the Lawgiver; to thee, the heaven that contains Him who can be contained of none? For since thou, O holy virgin, hast dawned as a bright day upon the world and hast brought forth the Sun of Righteousness, that hateful horror of darkness has been chased away; the power of the tyrant has been broken, death hath been destroyed, hell swallowed up, and all enmity dissolved before the face of peace; noxious diseases depart now that salvation looks forth; and the whole universe has been filled with the pure and clear light of truth. To which things Solomon alludes in the Book of Canticles, and begins thus: "My beloved is mine, and I am his; he feeds among the lilies until the day break, and the shadows flee away." Since then, the God of gods hath appeared in Sion, and the splendor of His beauty hath appeared in Jerusalem; and "a light has sprung up for the righteous, and joy for those who are true of heart." According to the blessed David, the Perfecter and Lord of the perfected hath, by the Holy Spirit, called the teacher and minister of the law to minister and testify of those things which were done.

VI. Hence the aged Simeon, putting off the weakness of the flesh, and putting on the strength of hope, in the face of the law hastened to receive the Minister of the law, the Teacher with authority, the God of Abraham, the Protector of Isaac, the Holy One of Israel, the Instructor of Moses; Him, I say, who promised to show him His divine incarnation, as it were His hinder parts; Him who, in the midst of poverty, was rich; Him who in infancy was before the ages; Him who, though seen, was invisible; Him who in comprehension was incomprehensible; Him who, though in littleness, yet surpassed all magnitude—at one and the same time in the temple and in the highest heavens—on a royal throne, and on the chariot of the cherubim Him who is both above and below continuously; Him who is in the form of a servant, and in the form of God the Father; a subject, and yet King of all. He was entirely given up to desire, to hope, to joy; he was no longer his own, but His who had been looked for. The Holy Spirit had announced to him the joyful tidings, and before he reached the temple, carried aloft by the eyes of his understanding, as if even now he possessed what he had longed for, he exulted with joy. Being thus led on, and in his haste treading the air with his steps, he reaches the shrine hitherto held sacred; but, not heeding the temple, he stretches out his holy arms to the Ruler of the temple, chanting forth in song such strains as become the joyous occasion: I long for Thee, O Lord God of my fathers, and Lord of mercy, who hast deigned, of Thine own glory and goodness, which provides for all, of Thy gracious condescension, with which Thou inclines towards us, as a Mediator bringing peace, to establish harmony between earth and heaven. I seek Thee, the Great Author of all. With longing I expect Thee who, with Thy word, embraces all things. I wait for Thee, the Lord of life and death. For Thee I look, the Giver of the law, and the Successor of the law. I hunger for Thee, who quickens the dead; I thirst for Thee, who refreshes the weary; I desire Thee, the Creator and Redeemer of the world. Thou art our God, and Thee we adore; Thou art our holy Temple, and in Thee we pray; Thou art our Lawgiver, and Thee we obey; Thou art God of all things the First. Before Thee was no other god begotten of God the Father; neither after Thee shall there be any other son consubstantial and of one glory with the Father. And to know Thee is perfect righteousness, and to know Thy power is the root of immortality. Thou art He who, for our salvation, was made the head stone of the corner, precious and honorable, declared before to Sion. For all things are placed under Thee as their Cause and Author, as He who brought all things into being out of nothing, and gave to what was unstable a firm coherence; as the connecting Band and Preserver of that which has been brought into being; as the Framer of things by nature different; as He who, with wise and steady hand, holds the helm of the universe; as the very Principle of all good order; as the irrefragable Bond of concord and peace. For in Thee we live, and move, and have our being. Wherefore, O Lord my God, I will glorify Thee, I will praise Thy name; for Thou hast done wonderful things; Thy counsels of old are faithfulness and truth; Thou art clothed with majesty and honor. For what is more splendid for a king than a purple robe embroidered around with flowers, and a shining diadem? Or what for God, who delights in man, is more magnificent than this merciful assumption of the manhood, illuminating with its resplendent rays those who sit in darkness and the shadow of death? Fitly did that temporal king and Thy servant once sing of Thee as the King Eternal, saying, Thou art fairer than the children of men, who amongst men art very God and man. For Thou hast girt, by Thy incarnation, Thy loins with righteousness, and anointed Thy veins with faithfulness, who Thyself art very righteousness and truth, the joy and exultation of all. Therefore rejoice with me this day, ye heavens, for the Lord hath showed mercy to His people. Yea, let the clouds drop the dew of righteousness upon the world; let the foundations of the earth sound a trumpet-blast to those in Hades, for the resurrection of them that sleep is come. Let the earth also cause compassion to spring up to its inhabitants; for I am filled with comfort; I am exceeding joyful since I have seen Thee, the Savior of men.

VII. While the old man was thus exultant, and rejoicing with exceeding great and holy joy, that which had before been spoken of in a figure by the prophet Isaiah, the holy mother of God now manifestly fulfilled. For taking, as from a pure and undefiled altar, that coal living and ineffable, with man's flesh invested, in the embrace of her sacred hands, as it were with the tongs, she held Him out to that just one, addressing and exhorting him, as it seems to me, in words to this effect: Receive, O reverend senior, thou of priests the most excellent, receive the Lord, and reap the full fruition of that hope of thine which is not left widowed and desolate. Receive, thou of men the most illustrious, the unfailing treasure, and those riches which can never be taken away. Take to thine embrace, O thou of men most wise, that unspeakable might, that unsearchable power, which can alone support thee. Embrace, thou minister of the temple, the Greatness infinite, and the Strength incomparable. Fold thyself around Him who is the very life itself, and live, O thou of men most venerable. Cling closely to incorruption and be renewed, O thou of men most righteous. Not too bold is the attempt; shrink not from it then, O thou of men most holy. Satiate thyself with Him thou hast longed for, and take thy delight in Him who has been given, or rather who gives Himself to thee, O thou of men most divine. Joyfully draw thy light, O thou of men most pious, from the Sun of Righteousness, that gleams around thee through the unsullied mirror of the flesh. Fear not His gentleness, nor let His clemency terrify thee, O thou of men most blessed. Be not afraid of His lenity, nor shrink from His kindness, O thou of men most modest. Join thyself to Him with alacrity, and delay not to obey Him. That which is spoken to thee, and held out to thee, savors not of over-boldness. Be not then reluctant, O thou of men the most decorous. The flame of the grace of my Lord does not consume, but illuminates thee, O thou of men most just. Let the bush which set forth me in type, with respect to the verity of that fire which yet had no subsistence, teach thee this, O thou who art in the law the best instructed. Let that furnace which was as it were a breeze distilling dew persuade thee, O master, of the dispensation of this mystery. Then, beside all this, let my womb be a proof to thee, in which He was contained, who in naught else was ever contained, of the substance of which the incarnate Word yet deigned to become incarnate. The blast of the trumpet does not now terrify those who approach, nor a second time does the mountain all on smoke cause terror to those who draw nigh, nor indeed does the law punish relentlessly those who would boldly touch. What is here present speaks of love to man; what is here apparent, of the Divine condescension. Thankfully, then, receive the God who comes to thee, for He shall take away thine iniquities, and thoroughly purge thy sins. In thee, let the cleansing of the world first, as in type, have place. In thee, and by thee, let that justification which is of grace become known beforehand to the Gentiles. Thou art worthy of the quickening first-fruits. Thou hast made good use of the law. Use grace henceforth. With the letter thou hast grown weary; in the spirit be renewed. Put off that which is old, and clothe thyself with that which is new. For of these matters I think not that thou art ignorant.

VIII. Upon all this that righteous man, waxing bold and yielding to the exhortation of the mother of God, who is the handmaid of God in regard to the things which pertain to men, received into his aged arms Him who in infancy was yet the Ancient of days, and blessed God, and said, "Lord, now lets Thou Thy servant depart in peace, according to Thy word: for mine eyes have seen Thy salvation, which Thou hast prepared before the face of all people; a light to lighten the Gentiles, and the glory of Thy people Israel." I have received from Thee a joy unmixed with pain. Do thou, O Lord, receive me rejoicing, and singing of Thy mercy and compassion. Thou hast given unto me this joy of heart. I render unto Thee with gladness my tribute of thanksgiving. I have known the power of the love of God. Since, for my sake, God of Thee begotten, in a manner ineffable, and without corruption, has become man. I have known the inexplicable greatness of Thy love and care for us, for Thou hast sent forth Thine own bowels to come to our deliverance. Now, at length, I understand what I had from

Solomon learned: "Strong as death is love: for by it shall the sting of death be done away, by it shall the dead see life, by it shall even death learn what death is, being made to cease from that dominion which over us he exercised. By it, also, shall the serpent, the author of our evils, be taken captive and overwhelmed." Thou hast made known to us, O Lord, Thy salvation, causing to spring up for us the plant of peace, and we shall no longer wander in error. Thou hast made known to us, O Lord, that Thou hast not unto the end overlooked Thy servants; neither hast Thou, O beneficent One, forgotten entirely the works of Thine hands. For out of Thy compassion for our low estate Thou hast shed forth upon us abundantly that goodness of Thine which is inexhaustible, and with Thy very nature cognate, having redeemed us by Thine only begotten Son, who is unchangeably like to Thee, and of one substance with Thee; judging it unworthy of Thy majesty and goodness to entrust to a servant the work of saving and benefiting Thy servants, or to cause that those who had offended should be reconciled by a minister. But by means of that light, which is of one substance with Thee, Thou hast given light to those that sat in darkness and in the shadow of death, in order that in Thy light they might see the light of knowledge; and it has seemed good to Thee, by means of our Lord and Creator, to fashion us again unto immortality; and Thou hast graciously given unto us a return to Paradise by means of Him who separated us from the joys of Paradise; and by means of Him who hath power to forgive sins Thou hast blotted out the handwriting which was against us. Lastly, by means of Him who is a partaker of Thy throne and who cannot be separated from Thy divine nature, Thou hast given unto us the gift of reconciliation and access unto Thee with confidence in order that, by the Lord who recognizes the sovereign authority of none, by the true and omnipotent God, the subscribed sanction, as it were, of so many and such great blessings might constitute the justifying gifts of grace to be certain and indubitable rights to those who have obtained mercy. And this very thing the prophet before had announced in the words: No ambassador, nor angel, but the Lord Himself saved them; because He loved them, and spared them, and He took them up, and exalted them. And all this was, not of works of righteousness which we have done, nor because we loved Thee,—for our first earthly forefather, who was honorably entertained, in the delightful abode of Paradise, despised Thy divine and saving commandment, and was judged unworthy of that life-giving place, and mingling his seed with the bastard off-shoots of sin, he rendered it very weak;—but Thou, O Lord, of Thine own self, and of Thine ineffable love toward the creature of Thine hands, hast confirmed Thy mercy toward us, and, pitying our estrangement from Thee, hast moved Thyself at the sight of our degradation to take us into compassion. Hence, for the future, a joyous festival is established for us of the race of Adam, because the first Creator of Adam of His own free-will has become the Second Adam. And the brightness of the Lord our God hath come down to sojourn with us, so that we see God face to face, and are saved. Therefore, O Lord, I seek of Thee to be allowed to depart. I have seen Thy salvation; let me be delivered from the bent yoke of the letter. I have seen the King Eternal, to whom no other succeeds; let me be set free from this servile and burdensome chain. I have seen Him who is by nature my Lord and Deliverer; may I obtain, then, His decree for my deliverance. Set me free from the yoke of condemnation, and place me under the yoke of justification. Deliver me from the yoke of the curse, and of the letter that kills; and enroll me in the blessed company of those who, by the grace of this Thy true Son, who is of equal glory and power with Thee, have been received into the adoption of sons.

IX. Let then, says he, what I have thus far said in brief, suffice for the present as my offering of thanks to God. But what shall I say to thee, O mother-virgin and virgin-mother? For the praise even of her who is not man's work exceeds the power of man. Wherefore the dimness of my poverty I will make bright with the splendor of the gifts of the spirits that around thee shine, and offering to thee of thine own, from the immortal meadows I will pluck a garland for thy sacred and divinely crowned head. With thine ancestral hymns will I greet thee, O daughter of David, and mother of the Lord and God of David. For it were both base and inauspicious to adorn thee, who in thine own glory excels with that which belongs unto another. Receive, therefore, O lady most benignant, gifts precious, and such as are fitted to thee alone, O thou who art exalted above all generations, and who, amongst all created things, both visible and invisible, shines forth as the most honorable. Blessed is the root of Jesse, and thrice blessed is the house of David, in which thou hast sprung up. God is in the midst of thee, and thou shalt not be moved, for the Most High hath made holy the place of His tabernacle. For in thee the covenants and oaths made of God unto the fathers have received a most glorious fulfilment, since by thee the Lord hath appeared, the God of hosts with us. That bush which could not be touched, which beforehand shadowed forth thy figure endowed with divine majesty, bare God without being consumed, who manifested Himself to the prophet just so far as He willed to be seen. Then, again, that hard and rugged rock, which imaged forth the grace and refreshment which has sprung out from thee for all the world, brought forth abundantly in the desert out of its thirsty sides a healing draught for the fainting people. Yea, moreover, the rod of the priest which, without culture, blossomed forth in fruit, the pledge and earnest of a perpetual priesthood, furnished no contemptible symbol of thy supernatural child-bearing. What, moreover? Hath not the mighty Moses expressly declared, that on account of these types of thee, hard to be understood, he delayed longer on the mountain, in order that he might learn, O holy one, the mysteries that with thee are connected? For being commanded to build the ark as a sign and similitude of this thing, he was not negligent in obeying the command, although a tragic occurrence happened on his descent from the mount; but having made it in size five cubits and a half, he appointed it to be the receptacle of the law, and covered it with the wings of the cherubim, most evidently pre-signifying thee, the mother of God, who hast conceived Him without corruption, and in an ineffable manner brought forth Him who is Himself, as it were, the very consistence of incorruption, and that within the limits of the five and a half circles of the world. On thy account, and the undefiled Incarnation of God, the Word, which by thee had place for the sake of that flesh which immutably and indivisibly remains with Him forever. The golden pot also, as a most certain type, preserved the manna contained in it, which in other cases was changed day by day, unchanged, and keeping fresh for ages. The prophet Elijah likewise, as prescient of thy chastity, and being emulous of it through the Spirit, bound around him the crown of that fiery life, being by the divine decree adjudged superior to death. Thee also, prefiguring his successor Elisha, having been instructed by a wise master, and anticipating thy presence who was not yet born, by certain sure indications of the things that would have place hereafter, ministered help and healing to those who were in need of it, which was of a virtue beyond nature; now with a new cruse, which contained healing salt, curing the deadly waters, to show that the world was to be recreated by the mystery manifested in thee; now with unleavened meal, in type responding to thy child-bearing, without being defiled by the seed of man, banishing from the food the bitterness of death; and then again, by efforts which transcended nature, rising superior to the natural elements in the Jordan, and thus exhibiting, in signs beforehand, the descent of our Lord into Hades, and His wonderful deliverance of those who were held fast in corruption. For all things yielded and succumbed to that divine image which prefigured thee.

X. But why do I digress, and lengthen out my discourse, giving it the rein with these varied illustrations, and that when the truth of thy matter stands like a column before the eye, in which it were better and more profitable to luxuriate and delight in? Wherefore, bidding adieu to the spiritual narrations and wondrous deeds of the saints throughout all ages, I pass on to thee who art always to be had in remembrance, and who holds the helm, as it were, of this festival.

Blessed art thou, all-blessed, and to be desired of all. Blessed of the Lord is thy name, full of divine grace, and grateful exceedingly to God, mother of God, thou that gives light to the faithful. Thou art the circumscription, so to speak, of Him who cannot be circumscribed; the root of the most beautiful flower; the mother of the Creator; the nurse of the Nourisher; the circumference of Him who embraces all things; the upholder of Him who upholds all things by His word; the gate through which God appears in the flesh; the tongs of that cleansing coal; the bosom in small of that bosom which is all-containing; the fleece of wool, the mystery of which cannot be solved; the well of Bethlehem, that reservoir of life which David longed for, out of which the draught of immortality gushed forth; the mercy-seat from which God in human form was made known unto men; the spotless robe of Him who clothes Himself with light as with a garment. Thou hast lent to God, who stands in need of nothing, that flesh which He had not, in order that the Omnipotent might become that which it was his good pleasure to be. What is more splendid than this? What than this is more sublime? He who fills earth and heaven, whose are all things, has become in need of thee, for thou hast lent to God that flesh which He had not. Thou hast clad the Mighty One with that beauteous panoply of the body by which it has become possible for Him to be seen by mine eyes. And I, in order that I might freely approach to behold Him, have received that by which all the fiery darts of the wicked shall be quenched. Hail! hail! Mother and handmaid of God. Hail! Hail! Thou to whom the great Creditor of all is a debtor. We are all debtors to God, but to thee He is Himself indebted.

For He who said, "Honor thy father and thy mother," will have most assuredly, as Himself willing to be proved by such proofs, kept inviolate that grace, and His own decree towards her who ministered to Him that nativity to which He voluntarily stooped, and will have glorified with a divine honor her whom He, as being without a father, even as she was without a husband, Himself has written down as mother. Even so must these things be. For the hymns which we offer to thee, O thou most holy and admirable habitation of God, are no merely useless and ornamental words. Nor, again, is thy spiritual laudation mere secular trifling, or the shouting of a false flattery, O thou who of God art praised; thou who to God gives suck; who by nativity gives unto mortals their beginning of being, but they are of clear and evident truth. But the time would fail us, ages and succeeding generations too, to render unto thee thy fitting salutation as the mother of the King Eternal, even as somewhere the illustrious prophet says, teaching us how incomprehensible thou art. How great is the house of God, and how large is the place of His possession! Great, and hath none end, high and unmeasurable. For verily, verily, this prophetic oracle, and most true saying, is concerning thy majesty; for thou alone hast been thought worthy to share with God the things of God; who hast alone borne in the flesh Him, who of God the Father was the Eternally and Only-Begotten. So do they truly believe who hold fast to the pure faith.

XI. But for the time that remains, my most attentive hearers, let us take up the old man, the receiver of God, and our pious teacher, who hath put in here, as it were, in safety from that virginal sea, and let us refresh him, both satisfied as to his divine longing, and conveying to us this most blessed theology; and let us ourselves follow out the rest of our discourse, directing our course unerringly with reference to our prescribed end, and that under the guidance of God the Almighty, so shall we not be found altogether unfruitful and unprofitable as to what is required of us. When, then, to these sacred rites, prophecy and the priesthood had been jointly called, and that pair of just ones elected of God—Simeon, I mean, and Anna, bearing in themselves most evidently the images of both peoples—had taken their station by the side of that glorious and virginal throne,—for by the old man was represented the people of Israel, and the law now waxing old; whilst the widow represents the Church of the Gentiles, which had been up to this point a widow,—the old man, indeed, as personating the law, seeks dismissal; but the widow, as personating the Church, brought her joyous confession of faith and spoke of Him to all that looked for redemption in Jerusalem, even as the things that were spoken of both have been appositely and excellently recorded, and quite in harmony with the sacred festival. For it was fitting and necessary that the old man who knew so accurately that decree of the law, in which it is said: Hear Him, and every soul that will not hearken unto Him shall be cut off from His people, should seek a peaceful discharge from the tutorship of the law; for in truth it were insolence and presumption, when the king is present and addressing the people, for one of his attendants to make a speech over against him, and that to this man his subjects should incline their ears. It was necessary, too, that the widow who had been increased with gifts beyond measure, should in festal strains return her thanks to God; and so the things which there took place were agreeable to the law. But, for what remains, it is necessary to inquire how, since the prophetic types and figures bear, as has been shown, a certain analogy and relation to this prominent feast, it is said that the house was filled with smoke. Nor does the prophet say this incidentally, but with significance, speaking of that cry of the Thrice-Holy, uttered by the heavenly seraphs. You will discover the meaning of this, my attentive hearer, if you do but take up and examine what follows upon this narration: For hearing, he says, ye shall hear, and shall not understand; and seeing, ye shall see, and not perceive. When, therefore, the foolish Jewish children had seen the glorious wonders which, as David sang, the Lord had performed in the earth, and had seen the sign from the depth and from the height meeting together, without division or confusion; as also Isaiah had before declared, namely, a mother beyond nature, and an offspring beyond reason; an earthly mother and a heavenly son; a new taking of man's nature, I say, by God, and a child-bearing without marriage; what in creation's circuit could be more glorious and more to be spoken of than this! Yet when they had seen this it was all one as if they had not seen it; they closed their eyes, and in respect of praise were supine. Therefore the house in which they boasted was filled with smoke.

XII. And in addition to this, when besides the spectacle, and even beyond the spectacle, they heard an old man, very righteous, very worthy of credit, worthy also of emulation, inspired by the Holy Spirit, a teacher of the law, honored with the priesthood, illustrious in the gift of prophecy, by the hope which he had conceived of Christ, extending the limits of life, and putting off the debt of death—when they saw him, I say, leaping for joy, speaking words of good omen, quite transformed with gladness of heart, entirely rapt in a divine and holy ecstasy; who from a man had been changed into an angel by a godly change, and, for the immensity of his joy, chanted his hymn of thanksgiving, and openly proclaimed the "Light to lighten the Gentiles, and the glory of Thy people Israel." Not even then were they willing to hear what was placed within their hearing, and held in veneration by the heavenly beings themselves; wherefore the house in which they boasted was filled with smoke. Now smoke is a sign and sure evidence of wrath; as it is written, "There went up a smoke in His anger, and fire from His countenance devoured;" and in another place, "Amongst the disobedient people shall the fire burn," which plainly, in the revered Gospels, our Lord signified, when He said to the Jews, "Behold your house is left unto you desolate." Also, in another place, "The king sent forth his armies, and destroyed those murderers, and burnt up their city." Of such a nature was the adverse reward of the Jews for their unbelief, which caused them to refuse to pay to the Trinity the tribute of praise. For after that the ends of the earth were sanctified, and the mighty house of the Church was filled, by the proclamation of the Thrice Holy, with the glory of the Lord, as the great waters cover the seas, there happened to them the things which before had been declared, and the beginning of prophecy was confirmed by its issue, the preacher of truth signifying, as has been said, by the Holy Spirit, as it were in an example, the dreadful destruction which was to come upon them, in the words: "In the year in which king Uzziah died, I saw the Lord"—Uzziah, doubtless, as an apostate, being taken as the representative of the whole apostate body—the head of which he certainly was—who also, paying the penalty due to his presumption, carried on his forehead, as upon a brazen statue, the divine vengeance engraved, by the loathsomeness of leprosy, exhibiting to all the retribution of their loathsome impiety. Wherefore with divine wisdom did he, who had foreknowledge of these events, oppose the bringing in of the thankful Anna to the casting out of the ungrateful synagogue. Her very name also pre-signifies the Church, that by the grace of Christ and God is justified in baptism. For Anna is, by interpretation, grace.

    XIII. But here, as in port, putting in the vessel that bears the ensign of the cross, let us reef the sails of our oration, in order that it may be with itself commensurate. Only first, in as few words as possible, let us salute the city of the Great King together with the whole body of the Church, as being present with them in spirit, and keeping holy-day with the Father, and the brethren most held in honor there. Hail, thou city of the Great King, in which the mysteries of our salvation are consummated. Hail, thou heaven upon earth, Sion, the city that is forever faithful unto the Lord. Hail, and shine thou Jerusalem, for thy light is come, the Light Eternal, the Light forever enduring, the Light Supreme, the Light Immaterial, the Light of one substance with God and the Father, the Light which is in the Spirit, and in which is the Father; the Light which illumines the ages; the Light which gives light to mundane and supramundane things, Christ our very God. Hail, city sacred and elect of the Lord. Joyfully keep thy festal days, for they will not multiply so as to wax old and pass away. Hail, thou city most happy, for glorious things are spoken of thee; thy priest shall be clothed with righteousness, and thy saints shall shout for joy, and thy poor shall be satisfied with bread. Hail! Rejoice, O Jerusalem, for the Lord reigned in the midst of thee. That Lord, I say, who in His simple and immaterial Deity, entered our nature, and of the virgin's womb became ineffably incarnate; that Lord, who was partaker of nothing else save the lump of Adam, who was by the serpent tripped up. For the Lord laid not hold of the seed of angels—those, I say, who fell not away from that beauteous order and rank that was assigned to them from the beginning. To us He condescended, that Word who was always with the Father co-existent God. Nor, again, did He come into the world to restore; nor will He restore, as has been imagined by some impious advocates of the devil, those wicked demons who once fell from light; but when the Creator and Framer of all things had, as the most divine Paul says, laid hold of the seed of Abraham, and through him of the whole human race, He was made man forever, and without change, in order that by His fellowship with us, and our joining on to Him, the ingress of sin into us might be stopped, its strength being broken by degrees, and itself as wax being melted, by that fire which the Lord, when He came, sent upon the earth. Hail to thee, thou Catholic Church, which hast been planted in all the earth, and do thou rejoice with us. Fear not, little flock, the storms of the enemy, for it is your Father's good pleasure to give you the kingdom, and that you should tread upon the necks of your enemies. Hail, and rejoice, thou that was once barren, and without seed unto godliness, but who hast now many children of faith. Hail, thou people of the Lord, thou chosen generation, thou royal priesthood, thou holy nation, thou peculiar people—show forth His praises who hath called you out of darkness into His marvelous light; and for His mercies glorify Him.

XIV. Hail to thee forever, thou virgin mother of God, our unceasing joy, for unto thee do I again return. Thou art the beginning of our feast; thou art its middle and end; the pearl of great price that belongs unto the kingdom; the fat of every victim, the living altar of the bread of life. Hail, thou treasure of the love of God. Hail, thou fount of the Son's love for man. Hail, thou overshadowing mount of the Holy Ghost. Thou gleamed, sweet gift-bestowing mother, of the light of the sun; thou gleamed with the insupportable fires of a most fervent charity, bringing forth in the end that which was conceived of thee before the beginning, making manifest the mystery hidden and unspeakable, the invisible Son of the Father—the Prince of Peace, who in a marvelous manner showed Himself as less than all littleness. Wherefore, we pray thee, the most excellent among women, who boasts in the confidence of thy maternal honors, that thou would unceasingly keep us in remembrance. O holy mother of God, remember us, I say, who make our boast in thee, and who in hymns august celebrate the memory, which will ever live, and never fade away. And do thou also, O honored and venerable Simeon, thou earliest host of our holy religion, and teacher of the resurrection of the faithful, be our patron and advocate with that Savior God, whom thou was deemed worthy to receive into thine arms. We, together with thee, sing our praises to Christ, who has the power of life and death, saying, Thou art the true Light, proceeding from the true Light; the true God, begotten of the true God; the one Lord, before Thine assumption of the humanity; that One nevertheless, after Thine assumption of it, which is ever to be adored; God of Thine own self and not by grace, but for our sakes also perfect man; in Thine own nature the King absolute and sovereign, but for us and for our salvation existing also in the form of a servant, yet immaculately and without defilement. For Thou who art incorruption hast come to set corruption free, that Thou might render all things uncorrupt. For Thine is the glory, and the power, and the greatness, and the majesty, with the Father and the Holy Spirit, for ever. Amen.

Oration on the Palms.

I. Blessed be God; let us proceed, brethren, from wonders to the miracles of the Lord, and as it were, from strength to strength. For just as in a golden chain the links are so intimately joined and connected together, as that the one holds the other, and is fitted on to it, and so carries on the chain—even so the miracles that have been handed down by the holy Gospels, one after the other, lead on the Church of God, which delights in festivity, and refresh it, not with the meat that perishes, but with that which endures unto everlasting life. Come then, beloved, and let us, too, with prepared hearts, and with ears intent, listen to what the Lord our God shall say unto us out of the prophets and Gospels concerning this most sacred feast. Verily, He will speak peace unto His people, and to His saints, and to those which turn their hearts unto Him. To-day, the trumpet-blast of the prophets have roused the world, and have made glad and filled with joyfulness the churches of God that are everywhere amongst the nations. And, summoning the faithful from the exercise of holy fasting, and from the palæstra, wherein they struggle against the lusts of the flesh, they have taught them to sing a new hymn of conquest and a new song of peace to Christ who giveth the victory. Come then, everyone, and let us rejoice in the Lord; O come, all ye people, and let us clap our hands, and make a joyful noise to God our Savior, with the voice of melody. Let no one be without portion in this grace; let no one come short of this calling; for the seed of the disobedient is appointed to destruction.—Let no one neglect to meet the King, lest he be shut out from the Bridegroom's chamber.—Let no one amongst us be found to receive Him with a sad countenance, lest he be condemned with those wicked citizens—the citizens, I mean, who refused to receive the Lord as King over them. Let us all come together cheerfully; let us all receive Him gladly, and hold our feast with all honesty. Instead of our garments, let us strew our hearts before Him. In psalms and hymns, let us raise to Him our shouts of thanksgiving; and, without ceasing, let us exclaim, "Blessed is He that cometh in the name of the Lord;" for blessed are they that bless Him, and cursed are they that curse Him. Again I will say it, nor will I cease exhorting you to good, Come, beloved, let us bless Him who is blessed, that we may be ourselves blessed of Him. Every age and condition does this discourse summon to praise the Lord; kings of the earth, and all people; princes, and all judges of the earth; both young men and maidens—and what is new in this miracle, the tender and innocent age of babes and sucklings hath obtained the first place in raising to God with thankful confession the hymn which was of God taught them in the strains in which Moses sang before to the people when they came forth out of Egypt—namely, "Blessed is He that cometh in the name of the Lord."

II. To-day, holy David rejoices with great joy, being by babes despoiled of his lyre, with whom also, in spirit, leading the dance, and rejoicing together, as of old, before the ark of God, he mingles musical harmony, and sweetly lisps out in stammering voice, Blessed is He that cometh in the name of the Lord. Of whom shall we inquire? Tell us, O prophet, who is this that cometh in the name of the Lord? He will say it is not my part to-day to teach you, for He hath consecrated the school to infants, who hath out of the mouth of babes and sucklings perfected praise to destroy the enemy and the avenger, in order that by the miracle of these the hearts of the fathers might be turned to the children, and the disobedient unto the wisdom of the just. Tell us, then, O children, whence is this, your beautiful and graceful contest of song? Who taught it you? Who instructed you? Who brought you together? What were your tablets? Who were your teachers? Do but you, they say, join us as our companions in this song and festivity, and you will learn the things which were by Moses and the prophet earnestly longed for. Since then the children have invited us, and have given unto us the right hand of fellowship, let us come, beloved, and ourselves emulate that holy chorus, and with the apostles, let us make way for Him who ascends over the heaven of heavens towards the East, and who, of His good pleasure, is upon the earth mounted upon an ass's colt. Let us, with the children, raise the branches aloft, and with the olive branches make glad applaud, that upon us also the Holy Spirit may breathe, and that in due order we may raise the God-taught strain: "Blessed is He that cometh in the name of the Lord; Hosanna in the highest." To-day, also, the patriarch Jacob keeps feast in spirit, seeing his prophecy brought to a fulfilment, and with the faithful adores the Father, seeing Him who bound his foal to the vine mounted upon an ass's colt. To-day the foal is made ready, the irrational exemplar of the Gentiles, who before were irrational, to signify the subjection of the people of the Gentiles; and the babes declare their former state of childhood, in respect of the knowledge of God, and their after perfecting, by the worship of God and the exercise of the true religion. To-day, according to the prophet, is the King of Glory glorified upon earth, and makes us, the inhabitants of earth, partakers of the heavenly feast, that He may show himself to be the Lord of both, even as He is hymned with the common praises of both. Therefore it was that the heavenly hosts sang, announcing salvation upon earth, "Holy, holy, holy, is the Lord God of hosts; the whole earth is full of His glory." And those below, joining in harmony with the joyous hymns of heaven, cried: "Hosanna in the highest; Hosanna to the Son of David." In heaven the doxology was raised, "Blessed be the glory of the Lord from His place;" and on earth was this caught up in the words, "Blessed is he that cometh in the name of the Lord."

III. But while these things were doing, and the disciples were rejoicing and praising God with a loud voice for all the mighty works that they had seen, saying, Blessed be the King that cometh in the name of the Lord; peace in heaven, and glory in the highest; the city began to inquire, saying, Who is this? Stirring up its hardened and inveterate envy against the glory of the Lord. But when thou hear me say the city, understand the ancient and disorderly multitude of the synagogue. They ungratefully and malignantly ask, Who is this? As if they had never yet seen their Benefactor, and Him whom divine miracles, beyond the power of man, had made famous and renowned; for the darkness comprehended not that unsetting light which shone in upon it. Hence quite appositely with respect to them hath the prophet Isaiah exclaimed, saying, Hear, ye deaf; and look, ye blind, that ye may see. And who is blind, but my children? And deaf, but they that have the dominion over them? And the servants of the Lord have become blind; ye have often seen, but ye observed not; your ears are opened, yet ye hear not. See, beloved, how accurate are these words; how the Divine Spirit, who Himself sees beforehand into the future, has by His saints foretold of things future as if they were present. For these thankless men saw, and by means of His miracles handled the wonder-working God, and yet remained in unbelief. They saw a man, blind from his birth, proclaiming to them the God who had restored his sight. They saw a paralytic, who had grown up, as it were, and become one with his infirmity, at His bidding loosed from his disease. They saw Lazarus, who was made an exile from the region of death. They heard that He had walked on the sea. They heard of the wine that, without previous culture, was ministered; of the bread that was eaten at that spontaneous banquet; they heard that the demons had been put to flight; the sick restored to health. Their very streets proclaimed His deeds of wonder; their roads declared His healing power to those who journeyed on them. All Judea was filled with His benefit; yet now, when they hear the divine praises, they inquire, Who is this? O the madness of these falsely-named teachers! O incredulous fathers! O foolish seniors! O seed of the shameless Canaan, and not of Judah the devout! The children acknowledge their Creator, but their unbelieving parents said, Who is this? The age that was young and inexperienced sang praises to God, while they that had waxen old in wickedness inquired, Who is this? Sucklings praise His Divinity, while seniors utter blasphemies; children piously offer the sacrifice of praise, whilst profane priests are impiously indignant.

IV. O ye disobedient as regards the wisdom of the just, turn your hearts to your children. Learn the mysteries of God; the very thing itself which is being done bears witness that it is God that is thus hymned by uninstructed tongues. Search the Scriptures, as ye have heard from the Lord; for they are they which testify of Him, and be not ignorant of this miracle. Hear ye men without grace, and thankless, what good tidings the prophet Zechariah brings to you. He says, Rejoice greatly, O daughter of Zion; behold thy King cometh unto thee: just and having salvation; lowly, and riding upon the foal of an ass. Why do ye repel the joy? Why, when the sun shines, do ye love darkness? Why do ye against unconquerable peace meditate war? If, therefore, ye be the sons of Zion, join in the dance together with your children. Let the religious service of your children be to you a pretext for joy. Learn from them who was their Teacher; who called them together; whence was the doctrine; what means this new theology and old prophecy. And if no man hath taught them this, but of their own accord they raise the hymn of praise, then recognize the work of God, even as it is written in the law: "Out of the mouth of babes and sucklings hast Thou perfected praise." Redouble, therefore, your joy, that you have been made the fathers of such children who, under the teaching of God, have celebrated with their praises things unknown to their seniors. Turn your hearts to your children, and close not your eyes against the truth. But if you remain the same, and hearing, hear not, and seeing, perceive not, and to no purpose dissent from your children, then shall they be your judges according to the Savior's word. Well, therefore, even this thing also, together with others, has the prophet Isaiah spoken before of you, saying, Jacob shall not now be ashamed, neither shall his face now wax pale. But when they see their children doing my works, they shall for me sanctify My name, and sanctify the Holy

One of Jacob, and shall fear the God of Israel. They also that err in spirit shall come to understanding, and they that murmured shall learn obedience, and the stammering tongues shall learn to speak peace. Sees thou, O foolish Jew, how from the beginning of his discourse, the prophet declares confusion to you because of your unbelief. Learn even from him how he proclaims the God-inspired hymn of praise that is raised by your children, even as the blessed David hath declared beforehand; saying, Out of the mouth of babes and sucklings hast Thou perfected praise. Either then,—as is right,—claim the piety of your children for your own, or devoutly give your children unto us. We with them will lead the dance, and to the new glory will sing in concert the divinely inspired hymn.

V. Once, indeed, the aged Simeon met the Savior and received in his arms, as an infant, the Creator of the world, and proclaimed Him to be Lord and God; but now, in the place of foolish elders, children meet the Savior, even as Simeon did, and instead of their arms, strew under Him the branches of trees, and bless the Lord God seated upon a colt, as upon the cherubim, Hosanna to the son of David: Blessed is He that cometh in the name of the Lord; and together with these let us also exclaim, Blessed is He that cometh, God the King of Glory, who, for our sakes, became poor, yet, in His own proper estate, being ignorant of poverty, that with His bounty He might make us rich. Blessed is He who once came in humility, and who will hereafter come again in glory: at the first, lowly, and seated upon an ass's colt, and by infants extolled in order that it might be fulfilled which was written: Thy goings have been seen, O God; even the goings of my God, my King, in the sanctuary; but at the second time seated on the clouds, in terrible majesty, by angels and powers attended. O the mellifluous tongue of the children! O the sincere doctrine of those who are well pleasing to God! David in prophecy hid the spirit under the letter; children, opening their treasures, brought forth riches upon their tongues, and, in language full of grace, invited clearly all men to enjoy them. Therefore let us with them draw forth the unfading riches. In our bosoms insatiate, and in treasure-houses which cannot be filled, let us lay up the divine gifts. Let us exclaim without ceasing, Blessed is He that cometh in the name of the Lord! Very God, in the name of the Very God, the Omnipotent from the Omnipotent, the Son in the name of the Father. The true King from the true King, whose kingdom, even as His who begat Him, is with eternity, coeval and pre-existent to it. For this is common to both; nor does the Scripture attribute this honor to the Son, as if it came from another source, nor as if it had a beginning, or could be added to or diminished—away with the thought!—but as that which is His of right by nature, and by a true and proper possession. For the kingdom of the Father, of the Son, and of the Holy Ghost, is one, even as their substance is one and their dominion one. Whence also, with one and the same adoration, we worship the one Deity in three Persons, subsisting without beginning, uncreated, without end, and to which there is no successor. For neither will the Father ever cease to be the Father, nor again the Son to be the Son and King, nor the Holy Ghost to be what in substance and personality He is. For nothing of the Trinity will suffer diminution, either in respect of eternity, or of communion, or of sovereignty. For not on that account is the Son of God called king, because for our sakes He was made man, and in the flesh cast down the tyrant that was against us, having, by taking this upon Him, obtained the victory over its cruel enemy, but because He is always Lord and God; therefore it is that now, both after His assumption of the flesh and forever, He remains a king, even as He who begat Him. Speak not, O heretic, against the kingdom of Christ, lest thou dishonor Him who begat Him. If thou art faithful, in faith approach Christ, our very God, and not as using your liberty for a cloak of maliciousness. If thou art a servant, with trembling be subject unto thy Master; for he who fights against the Word is not a well-disposed servant, but a manifest enemy, as it is written: He that honored not the Son, honored not the Father which hath sent Him.

VI. But let us, beloved, return in our discourse to that point whence we digressed, exclaiming, Blessed is He that cometh in the name of the Lord: that good and kind Shepherd, voluntarily to lay down His life for His sheep. That just as hunters take by a sheep the wolves that devour sheep, even so the Chief Shepherd, offering Himself as man to the spiritual wolves and those who destroy the soul, may make His prey of the destroyers by means of that Adam who was once preyed on by them. Blessed is He that cometh in the name of the Lord: God against the devil; not manifestly in His might, which cannot be looked on, but in the weakness of the flesh, to bind the strong man that is against us. Blessed is He that cometh in the name of the Lord: the King against the tyrant; not with omnipotent power and wisdom, but with that which is accounted the foolishness of the cross, which hath reft his spoils from the serpent who is wise in wickedness. Blessed is He that cometh in the name of the Lord: the True One against the liar; the Savior against the destroyer; the Prince of Peace against him who stirs up wars; the Lover of mankind against the hater of mankind.

Blessed is He that cometh in the name of the Lord: the Lord to have mercy upon the creature of His hands. Blessed is He that cometh in the name of the Lord: the Lord to save man who had wandered in error; to put away error; to give light to those who are in darkness; to abolish the imposture of idols; in its place to bring in the saving knowledge of God; to sanctify the world; to drive away the abomination and misery of the worship of false gods. Blessed is He that cometh in the name of the Lord: the one for the many; to deliver the poor out of the hands of them that are too strong for him, yea, the poor and needy from him that spoiled him. Blessed is He that cometh in the name of the Lord, to pour wine and oil upon him who had fallen amongst thieves, and had been passed by. Blessed is He that cometh in the name of the Lord: to save us by Himself, as says the prophet; no ambassador, nor angel, but the Lord Himself saved us. Therefore we also bless Thee, O Lord; Thou with the Father and the Holy Spirit art blessed before the worlds and forever. Before the world, indeed, and until now being devoid of body, but now and forever henceforth possessed of that divine humanity which cannot be changed, and from which Thou art never divided.

VII. Let us look also at what follows. What says the most divine evangelist? When the Lord had entered into the temple, the blind and the lame came to Him; and He healed them. And when the chief priests and Pharisees saw the wonderful things that He did, and the children crying, and saying, Hosanna to the Son of David: Blessed is He that cometh in the name of the Lord, they brooked not this honor that was paid Him, and therefore they came to Him, and thus spoke, Hears Thou not what these say? As if they said, Art Thou not grieved at hearing from these innocents things which befit God, and God alone? Has not God of old made it manifest by the prophet, "My glory will I not give unto another;" and how dost Thou, being a man, make Thyself God? But what to this answers the longsuffering One, He who is abundant in mercy, and slow to wrath? He bears with these frenzied ones; with an apology He keeps their wrath in check; in His turn He calls the Scriptures to their remembrance; He brings forward testimony to what is done, and shrinks not from inquiry. Wherefore He says, Have ye never heard Me saying by the prophet, Then shall ye know that I am He that doth speak? Nor again, Out of the mouth of babes and sucklings hast Thou perfected praise because of Thine enemies, that Thou might still the enemy and the avenger? Which without doubt are ye, who give heed unto the law, and read the prophets, while yet ye despise Me who, both by the law and the prophets, have been beforehand proclaimed. You think, indeed, under a presence of piety, to avenge the glory of God, not understanding that he that despises Me despises My Father also. I came forth from God, and am come into the world, and My glory is the glory of My Father also. Even thus these foolish ones, being convinced by our Savior-God, ceased to answer Him again, the truth stopping their mouths; but adopting a new and foolish device, they took counsel against Him. But let us sing, Great is our Lord, and great is His power; and of His understanding there is no number. For all this was done that the Lamb and Son of God, that taketh away the sins of the world, might, of His own will, and for us, come to His saving Passion, and might be recognized, as it were, in the market and place of selling; and that those who bought Him might for thirty pieces of silver covenant for Him who, with His life-giving blood, was to redeem the world; and that Christ, our Passover, might be sacrificed for us, in order that those who were sprinkled with His precious blood, and sealed on their lips, as the posts of the door, might escape from the darts of the destroyer; and that Christ having thus suffered in the flesh, and having risen again the third day, might, with equal honor and glory with the Father and the Holy Ghost, be by all created things equally adored; for to Him every knee shall bow, of things in heaven, and things in earth, and things under the earth, sending up glory to Him, for ever and ever. Amen.

Elucidations.

The candid Dupin says that we owe this to Père Combefis, on the authority of a ms. in the Royal Library of Paris. It appeared in Sir Henry Savile's edition of Chrysostom ascribed to that Father. Dupin doubts as to parts of this homily, if not as to the whole. He adds, "The style of Methodius is Asiatic, diffuse, swelling, and abounding in epithet. His expressions are figurative, and the turn of his sentences artificial. He is full of similitudes and far-fetched allegories. His thoughts are mysterious, and he uses many words to say a few things." His doctrine, apart from these faults, is sound, and free from some errors common to the ancients: such faults as I have frequently apologized for in Origen, whom Methodius so generally condemns.

Three Fragments from the Homily on the Cross and Passion of Christ.

I.

Methodius, Bishop, to those who say: What doth it profit us that the Son of God was crucified upon earth, and made man? And wherefore did He endure to suffer in the manner of the cross, and not by some other punishment? And what was the advantage of the cross?

Christ, the Son of God, by the command of the Father, became conversant with the visible creature, in order that, by overturning the dominion of the tyrants, the demons, that is, He might deliver our souls from their dreadful bondage, by reason of which our whole nature, intoxicated by the draughts of iniquity, had become full of tumult and disorder, and could by no means return to the remembrance of good and useful things. Wherefore, also, it was the more easily carried away to idols, inasmuch as evil had overwhelmed it entirely, and had spread over all generations, on account of the change which had come over our fleshy tabernacles in consequence of disobedience; until Christ, the Lord, by the flesh in which He lived and appeared, weakened the force of Pleasure's onslaughts, by means of which the infernal powers that were in arms against us reduced our minds to slavery, and freed mankind from all their evils. For with this end the Lord Jesus both wore our flesh, and became man, and by the divine dispensation was nailed to the cross; in order that by the flesh in which the demons had proudly and falsely feigned themselves gods, having carried our souls captive unto death by deceitful wiles, even by this they might be overturned, and discovered to be no gods. For he prevented their arrogance from raising itself higher, by becoming man; in order that by the body in which the race possessed of reason had become estranged from the worship of the true God, and had suffered injury, even by the same receiving into itself in an ineffable manner the

Word of Wisdom, the enemy might be discovered to be the destroyers and not the benefactors of our souls. For it had not been wonderful if Christ, by the terror of His divinity, and the greatness of His invincible power, had reduced to weakness the adverse nature of the demons. But since this was to cause them greater grief and torment, for they would have preferred to be overcome by one stronger than themselves, therefore it was that by a man He procured the safety of the race; in order that men, after that very Life and Truth had entered into them in bodily form, might be able to return to the form and light of the Word, overcoming the power of the enticements of sin; and that the demons, being conquered by one weaker than they, and thus brought into contempt, might desist from their over-bold confidence, their hellish wrath being repressed. It was for this mainly that the cross was brought in, being erected as a trophy against iniquity, and a deterrent from it, that henceforth man might be no longer subject to wrath, after that he had made up for the defeat which, by his disobedience, he had received, and had lawfully conquered the infernal powers, and by the gift of God had been set free from every debt. Since, therefore, the first-born Word of God thus fortified the manhood in which He tabernacle with the armor of righteousness, He overcame, as has been said, the powers that enslaved us by the figure of the cross, and showed forth man, who had been oppressed by corruption, as by a tyrant power, to be free, with unfettered hands. For the cross, if you wish to define it, is the confirmation of the victory, the way by which God to man descended, the trophy against material spirits, the repulsion of death, the foundation of the ascent to the true day; and the ladder for those who are hastening to enjoy the light that is there, the engine by which those who are fitted for the edifice of the Church are raised up from below, like a stone four square, to be compacted on to the divine Word. Hence it is that our kings, perceiving that the figure of the cross is used for the dissipating of every evil, have made *vexillas*, as they are called in the Latin language. Hence the sea, yielding to this figure, makes itself navigable to men. For every creature, so to speak, has, for the sake of liberty, been marked with this sign; for the birds which fly aloft, form the figure of the cross by the expansion of their wings; and man himself, also, with his hands outstretched, represents the same. Hence, when the Lord had fashioned him in this form, in which He had from the beginning framed him, He joined on his body to the Deity, in order that it might be henceforth an instrument consecrated to God, freed from all discord and want of harmony. For man cannot, after that he has been formed for the worship of God, and hath sung, as it were, the incorruptible song of truth, and by this hath been made capable of holding the Deity, being fitted to the lyre of life as the chords and strings, he cannot, I say, return to discord and corruption.

II.
The Same Methodius to Those Who are Ashamed of the Cross of Christ.

Some think that God also, whom they measure with the measure of their own feelings, judges the same thing that wicked and foolish men judge to be subjects of praise and blame, and that He uses the opinions of men as His rule and measure, not taking into account the fact that, by reason of the ignorance that is in them, every creature falls short of the beauty of God. For He draws all things to life by His Word, from their universal substance and nature. For whether He would have good, He Himself is the Very Good, and remains in Himself; or, whether the beautiful is pleasing to Him, since He Himself is the Only Beautiful, He beholds Himself, holding in no estimation the things which move the admiration of men. That, verily, is to be accounted as in reality the most beautiful and praiseworthy, which God Himself esteems to be beautiful, even though it be contemned and despised by all else—not that which men fancy to be beautiful. Whence it is, that although by this figure He hath willed to deliver the soul from corrupt affections, to the signal putting to shame of the demons, we ought to receive it, and not to speak evil of it, as being that which was given us to deliver us, and set us free from the chains which for our disobedience we incurred. For the Word suffered, being in the flesh affixed to the cross, that He might bring man, who had been deceived by error, to His supreme and godlike majesty, restoring him to that divine life from which he had become alienated. By this figure, in truth, the passions are blunted; the passion of the passions having taken place by the Passion, and the death of death by the death of Christ, He not having been subdued by death, nor overcome by the pains of the Passion. For neither did the Passion cast Him down from His equanimity, nor did death hurt Him, but He was in the passible remaining impassible, and in the mortal remaining immortal, comprehending all that the air, and this middle state, and the heaven above contained, and attempering the mortal to the immortal divinity. Death was vanquished entirely; the flesh being crucified to draw forth its immortality.

III.

The Same Methodius: How Christ the Son of God, in a Brief and Definite Time, Being Enclosed by the Body, and Existing Impassible, Became Obnoxious to the Passion.

For since this virtue was in Him, now it is of the essence of power to be contracted in a small space, and to be diminished, and again to be expanded in a large space, and to be increased. But if it is possible for Him to be with the larger extended, and to be made equal, and yet not with the smaller to be contracted and diminished, then power is not in Him. For if you say that this is possible to power, and that impossible, you deny it to be power; as being infirm and incapable with regard to the things which it cannot do. Nor again, further, will it ever contain any excellence of divinity with respect to those things which suffer change. For both man and the other animals, with respect to those things which they can effect, energize; but with respect to those things which they cannot perform, are weak, and fade away. Wherefore for this cause the Son of God was in the manhood enclosed, because this was not impossible to Him. For with power He suffered, remaining impassible; and He died, bestowing the gift of immortality upon mortals. Since the body, when struck or cut by a body, is just so far struck or cut as the striker strikes it, or he that cuts it cut it. For according to the rebound of the thing struck, the blow reflects upon the striker, since it is necessary that the two must suffer equally, both the agent and the sufferer. If, in truth, that which is cut, from its small size, does not correspond to that which cuts it, it will not be able to cut it at all. For if the subject body does not resist the blow of the sword, but rather yields to it, the operation will be void of effect, even as one sees in the thin and subtle bodies of fire and air; for in such cases the impetus of the more solid bodies is relaxed, and remains without effect. But if fire, or air, or stone, or iron, or anything which men use against themselves for the purposes of mutual destruction—if it is not possible to pierce or divide these, because of the subtle nature which they possess, why should not rather Wisdom remain invulnerable and impassible, in nothing injured by anything, even though it were conjoined to the body which was pierced and transfixed with nails, inasmuch as it is purer and more excellent than any other nature, if you except only that of God who begat Him?

Some Other Fragments of the Same Methodius.

I.

But, perhaps, since the friends of Job imagined that they understood the reason why he suffered such things, that just man, using a long speech to them, confesses that the wisdom of the divine judgment is incomprehensible, not only to him, but also to every man, and declares that this earthly region is not the fitting place for understanding the knowledge of the divine counsels. One might say, that perfect and absolute piety—a thing plainly divine, and of God alone given to man, is in this place called wisdom. But the sense of the words is as follows: God, he says, hath given great things unto men, sowing, as it were, in their nature the power of discovery, together with wisdom, and the faculty of art. And men having received this, dig metals out of the earth, and cultivate it; but that wisdom which is conjoined with piety, it is not possible in any place to discover. Man cannot obtain it from his own resources, nor can he give it unto others. Hence it was that the wise men of the Greeks, who in their own strength sought to search out piety, and the worship of the Deity, did not attain their end. For it is a thing, as we have said, which exceeds human strength, the gift and the grace of God; and therefore from the beginning, partly by visions, partly by the intervention of angels, partly by the discourses of the divinely-inspired prophets, God instructed man in the principles of true religion. Nay, moreover, that contemplative wisdom by which we are impelled to the arts, and to other pursuits, and with which we are all in common, just and unjust, alike endued, is the gift of God: if we have been made rational creatures, we have received this. Wherefore, also, in a former place it was said, as of a thing that is of God bestowed, "Is it not the Lord who teaches understanding and knowledge?"

II.
Observe that the Lord was not wont from the beginning to speak with man; but after that the soul was prepared, and exercised in many ways, and had ascended into the height by contemplation, so far as it is possible for human nature to ascend, then is it His wont to speak, and to reveal His Word unto those who have attained unto this elevation. But since the whirlwind is the producer of the tempests, and Job, in the tempest of his afflictions, had not made shipwreck of his faith, but his constancy shone forth the rather; therefore it was that He who gave him an answer answered him by the whirlwind, to signify the tempest of calamity which had befallen him; but, because He changed the stormy condition of his affairs

into one of serene tranquility, He spoke to him not only by the whirlwind, but in clouds also.

III.

Many have descended into the deep, not so as to walk on it, but so as to be by its bonds restrained. Jesus alone walked on the deep, where there are no traces of walkers, as a free man. For He chose death, to which He was not subject, that He might deliver those who were the bond slaves of death; saying to the prisoners, "Go forth; and to them that are in darkness, show yourselves." With which, also, the things which follow are consistent.

IV.

Sees thou how, at the end of the contest, with a loud proclamation he declares the praises of the combatant, and discovers that which was in his afflictions hidden, in the words: "Thinks thou that I had else answered thee, but that thou should appear just?" This is the salve of his wounds, this the reward of his patience. For as to what followed, although he received double his former possessions, these may seem to have been given him by divine providence as small indeed, and for trifling causes, even though to some they may appear great.

Fragment, Uncertain.

Thou contends with Me, and sets thyself against Me, and opposes those who combat for Me. But where wert thou when I made the world? What wert thou then? Has thou yet, says He, fallen from thy mother? For there was darkness, in the beginning of the world's creation, He says, upon the face of the deep. Now this darkness was no created darkness, but one which of set purpose had place, by reason of the absence of light.

V.

But Methodius: The Holy Spirit, who of God is given to all men, and of whom Solomon said, "For Thine incorruptible Spirit is in all things," He receives for the conscience, which condemns the offending soul.

VI. The Same Methodius.

I account it a greater good to be reproved than to reprove, inasmuch as it is more excellent to free oneself from evil than to free another.

VII. The Same Methodius.

Human nature cannot clearly perceive pure justice in the soul, since, as to many of its thoughts, it is but dim-sighted.

VIII. The Same Methodius.

Wickedness never could recognize virtue or its own self.

IX. The Same Methodius.

Justice, as it seems, is four square, on all sides equal and like.

The just judgment of God is accommodated to our affections; and such as our estate is, proportionate and similar shall the retribution be which is allotted us.

Two Fragments, Uncertain.

I.
The beginning of every good action has its foundation in our wills, but the conclusion is of God.

II.
Perhaps these three persons of our ancestors, being in an image the consubstantial representatives of humanity, are, as also Methodius thinks, types of the Holy and Consubstantial Trinity, the innocent and unbegotten Adam being the type and resemblance of God the Father Almighty, who is uncaused, and the cause of all; his begotten son shadowing forth the image of the begotten Son and Word of God; whilst Eve, that proceeded forth from Adam, signifies the person and procession of the Holy Spirit.

General Note.
_____

(*Vexillas,*—as they are called.)
It is very curious to note how certain ideas are inherited from the earliest Fathers, and travel down, as here, to find a new expression in a distant age. Here our author reflects Justin Martyr, and the *Labarum* itself is the outcrop of what Justin wrote to Antoninus Pius.

Find this and other great works of the early Church Fathers at lighthousechristianpublishing.com.

Our Father who art in heaven, hallowed be thy name.
Thy kingdom come, Thy will be done, on earth as it is in heaven.
Give us this day our daily bread and forgive us our trespasses as we forgive those who trespass against us.
And lead us not into temptation, but deliver us from evil, for Thine is the kingdom, the power and the glory. Forever and ever.

Amen

Methodius

Hail Mary full of grace, the Lord is with thee.
Blessed art thou amongst women and blessed is the fruit
of thy womb Jesus. Holy Mary mother of God, pray for us
sinners, now and the hour of our death.